I Will Teach You to Master Self-Discipline

Learn the 12 Rules to Take Back Control and Ownership of Your Life. Used by Navy SEALs, Champions, and Athletes. See the Effects in 3 Days or Less

Edgar D. Moranis

© Copyright 2019 - All rights reserved.

The content contained within this book may not be reproduced, duplicated or transmitted without direct written permission from the author or the publisher.

Under no circumstances will any blame or legal responsibility be held against the publisher, or author, for any damages, reparation, or monetary loss due to the information contained within this book. Either directly or indirectly.

Legal Notice:

This book is copyright protected. This book is only for personal use. You cannot amend, distribute, sell, use, quote or paraphrase any part, or the content within this book, without the consent of the author or publisher.

Disclaimer Notice:

Please note the information contained within this document is for educational and entertainment purposes only. All effort has been executed to present accurate, up to date, and reliable, complete information. No warranties of any kind are declared or implied. Readers acknowledge that the author is not engaging in the rendering of legal, financial, medical or professional advice. The content within this book has been derived from various sources. Please consult a licensed professional before attempting any techniques outlined in this book.

By reading this document, the reader agrees that under no circumstances is the author responsible for any losses, direct or indirect, which are incurred as a result of the use of information contained within this document, including, but not limited to, — errors, omissions, or inaccuracies.

Contents

Chapter 1:
Building Long-Term Success 1

Chapter 2:
Self-Discipline Fundamentals 17

Chapter 3:
Habits of Winners 26

Chapter 4:
Millionaire Self-Discipline Secrets 37

Chapter 5:
The Fool Proof Method to Achieve Your Goals 45

Chapter 6:
How to Break Bad Habits (The Right Way) 52

Chapter 7:
How to Force Productivity Out of Yourself 60

Chapter 8:
The Morning Routine Fix 69

Chapter 9:
Become More Productive in Less Time 76

Chapter 10:
Why You Procrastinate in Explained in 15 Minutes 84

Chapter 11:
Over Come Procrastination Through Self-Discipline.....................................93

Chapter 12:
Growth Mindset to Achieve Anything 102

Chapter 13:
The Future is Brighter Than You Think..111

Chapter 14:
My Number One Method to Build Self-Discipline (It Actually Works) 124

Chapter 1:
Building Long-Term Success

How can I do to become more successful? How can I be successful in all areas of my life, be it personal or professional? These are the questions that go around in most people's lives, always thinking of how they can become better in whatever they have set up their minds to. A lot of literature has been written concerning this subject over a very long time, but none of them have gone into details to give an elaborate formula that can make you become a man or woman of your dreams. That is why we have dedicated this first chapter of this book to enlighten you what foundation for success is and how to practice them in your life. In this chapter, we shall show you why self-discipline, overcoming temptation and procrastination, developing willpower and management of your time are the foundation for success.

Professional or personal development is solely dependent on you, and so you will need to be careful about how you carry yourself along if you are to achieve anything substantial in your life. You should note that no personal success can be attained or even a goal realized without working on your personal traits. I will encourage you to read on so that you may be enlightened.

Self-Discipline as A Foundation for Success

Self-discipline plays a significant role in personal success and achievements. In fact, no success can be realized in any area of your life without self-discipline. This is the single most essential personal attribute that is required for you to have any kind of personal excellence, career excellence, excellence in athletics and have an overall outstanding performance.

What Is Self-Discipline?

Self-discipline is known as the ability of an individual to control his or her impulses, desires, emotions, and behavior. Self-discipline can also be defined as the ability of a person to forego immediate pleasure and instant gratification so that he/she can gain satisfaction and fulfillment in the long-term. This comes from achieving higher and more important goals. When you possess self-discipline, you can make decisions, ensure actions and carry out your plan game despite the many obstacles, difficulties, and discomfort that you might face on the way.

However, living a disciplined life does not entail that you need to live a restrictive or limiting life. It does not also mean that you give up everything that gives you enjoyment, relaxation, and satisfaction. Self-discipline entails being able to focus both your mind and energies towards achieving specific set goals and stay put until they are achieved. It also gives you an opportunity to cultivate a mindset that will allow you to be ruled by choices that you have made deliberately as opposed to your emotions, bad habits or influence from other people. Being self-disciplined will enable you to achieve your goals in the set time-frame and have a life that is orderly and satisfying.

How Do You Develop Self-Discipline?

If you are dreaming of creating self-discipline like the one you see other people possess, all is not lost. Having that discipline is critical in the success of your career. It is paramount that you learn the tricks that will help you become more self-disciplined. Below we shall guide you on how you can develop your self-discipline and exceed the level that you are in currently:

Begin with Small Steps

No single process takes overnight only to mature. Just as it takes time for a person to learn new things or even build your muscles, so it requires time in developing self-discipline. For instance, if you are aiming at building muscles, you will need to take your time and train more. The more you engage in training, the more likely you will build your muscles and become strong. However, if your goal is to achieve a muscular body at once, you will be discouraged because it is not practical. Overworking yourself will only lead to setbacks due to injuries.

The same case applies when you aim at building your self-esteem. You will need to go through each step at a time in order to achieve your dreams. Therefore, the first step is to make the decision to progress and ensure you learn what is required to get to that destination. If you don't follow step by step towards gaining self-discipline, you will be overwhelmed when you experience too many changes you need to make at once. In the end, this may kill your intention of becoming self-disciplined.

Know What Motivates You and What Demotivates You
The first step in gaining self-discipline is to know and discover yourself. Sometimes it is easy to find we are being overcome by cravings and urges and so knowing areas in your life where you have no power no resist and avoid it will significantly help. For instance, if you know you can't avoid junks or other deep-fried foods, it will be advisable to stay away from them. Ensure you stay away from them to prevent them from luring you during the times of weakness.

Also, if you are aware that no matter how much pressure you put on yourself, it does not work, then you should put yourself in an environment that will promote the building of self-discipline as compared to a situation that will sabotage it. Stay away from temptations and stay close to items that soothe and encourage you such as motivating slogans and images of what you wish to attain.

It is essential to know what empowers and motivates you. Your will power will be directly proportional to your energy levels, and so you could play energetic songs to raise you up and laugh. Make yourself love what you are doing by staying energized. This will make it possible to put in place desirable and appropriate behaviors in your daily routine – which is what self-discipline entails.

Ensure Some Behaviors Are Your Routine

When you have settled on what is most important to you and what goals to put your effort on, have a daily routine that will enable you to attain them. For example, if you are working towards eating healthily or even losing weight, decide to take several servings of vegetables and fruits every day and do exercises for about thirty minutes a day. Ensure your daily habit is promoting the development of self-discipline. Consequently, you should keep away from bad, self-defeating practices, all that they may be. These practices can put you in a negative state of mind and derail your self-discipline. Also, avoid possessing a poor attitude because it is also a bad habit.

Exercise Self-Denial

When you are on a journey to developing self-discipline, you should learn to restrict some feelings, urges, and impulses. Train to act on what you believe is right, even if it is against you will. Skip some desserts on some evenings, limit your watching, and restrict yourself from yelling at anyone who irritates you. Always stop and think before you take steps and think about the outcomes of any action that you take. When you embrace the practice of self-restraint, it will enable you to promote a habit of keeping all things under control.

Involve Yourself in Sporting and Other Activities

Engaging in sports activities is among one of the best ways to promote self-discipline. Sports will train you to put in place your goals, focus both your emotional and mental energies, be fit physically and can get well along with others. Involving yourself in sports offers a situation where you work harder and put all your effort which in turn will enable you to integrate the same thought processes and discipline in your daily life.

Also practicing playing instruments to music can be another better way to practice self-discipline. There is an invaluable effort, repetition and application needed to when learning to play these instruments. When you attain self-discipline in any area, it will help reprogram your minds, and it will be easy to choose what is right instead of going for what is easy.

Get Inspired from The Right Places

There are many people out there who have achieved self-discipline and so learning from them will save a great deal. Be it in athletics, or any activity that you have decided to involve yourself in, make sure you are inspired by the people you admire. You should have a strong desire to do the right thing and go out of your way to achieve it. Some of the challenges you are facing today, have been experienced many people who have experienced the same and overcome and developing self-discipline is not exceptional.

Focus on The Rewards

There is nothing that brings a lot of satisfaction like accomplishing what you had aimed for. Exercise the techniques that high achievers and athletes' practice. See yourself in the future with your desired outcomes. You will see the benefits that you will get and always remind yourself of the price you ought to pay for you to get there.

Overcoming Temptation as A Foundation for Success

As you go through the past and review your goals, be keen to look at what has held you back from achieving your goals. One important question that you ought to ask yourself is what temptations you gave into. How can you stop yourself from letting temptations deter you from your goals?

Temptation can be defined as the desire to do something, particularly something wrong or unwise. It can also be a thing or course of actions that can attract or tempt you. This implies that once you have purposed to do something, for instance losing weight- you will meet every kind of temptation from every corner. You may go out with your friends for a party and have a glass of wine and skipping your gym sessions. You may even be finding yourself tempted to grab that piece of donut or cookies in the kitchen. Often our temptation is so habitual and usually unnoticed now, that you can quickly forget your focus goal. It is paramount for you to understand that these little amounts of food we need now or skipping the gym do not add anything towards where we aim to be. It is easy to get distracted that we fail to realize the temptations that face us.

The temptation that we face every day make us far from what we truly want. However, those temptations can make you strong when we push and refuse to give in to them. It is easy to be tempted to stray. The challenge comes when we decide to remain stronger.

Many times, at the start of your goal, you will strive to keep going. At that moment the temptation is stronger. When you experience the first signs of results, momentum will start to kick in; you will have more ability to fight temptation. Always remember that you are stronger than both the temptation and the will to give in. Human beings sometimes need to be challenged so that they can bring out their best.

How Do Temptations Work Against Your Goals?

It is important to note that all temptations follow a four-step process. It is paramount to learn it so that we can start being keen to where we might get caught by it.

A Desire That Comes from Within or A Feeling

Sometimes you might have a strong desire to revenge, control a situation or other people. It might even be an urge to feel appreciated or have pleasure. Many times, temptation begins in the mind. It is easy for you to negative minds, which can make it hard to achieve your targets. You might tell yourself – "it's only once", "it is good to go out with friends or colleagues because it will it will be fun", and the likes. This temptation will always start with your minds. Something will always be pushing us away from our objective or intentions. The circumstances that we found ourselves is not to blame for falling into temptation but our minds. Your mind will tell you it is okay if you do certain things. Therefore, for you to avoid giving in to temptation, you must start being cautious from the thoughts and imaginations that pulls you away from what you have planned.

Starting to Doubt

Sometimes you might find yourself doubting what you know. Your mind might tell you that skipping one day at the gym will not make a huge difference or I will take a day off because tomorrow I will get more work done. Your mind will argue that you deserve to be happy and to have what makes you happy, so go for it. Always be careful not to start doubting what you know. You should set your mind to fight the feeling of doubt. Remind yourself what you know and believe. For instance, remind yourself that skipping the gym for one day might make you lazy to do exercises the following day, having a day off today does not imply that tomorrow you will work extra hard or, eating sugar today might make you crave for more sugar. When you remind yourself of these things, you will not allow your minds to give in easily.

Be on The Lookout for Deception

You should remain alert lest your minds start lying to you. Remember you will always battle with temptations. Your thoughts might be tempted to think that all will be okay, you won't notice that one day off when you are being paid, everybody else is doing the same thing, or nobody will ever notice or know. Remember the saying what is done in the darkness will eventually reveal itself at a time. If you aim to lose weight and gain that impressive figure that you so much desire, you should stop eating the wrong diet if though you are tempted to do so. You are smart and have the power within you, and therefore you should not give in to that feeling that is whispering lies to you.

You Start Disobeying

If you give in to the three above, temptation has won. You will give in and begin doing things that will keep you away from your goals.

It is like a cycle. When you have sat down and review your goal for a week, month or year, ask yourself- what temptation have you fallen into? Which are the cravings and desires that arose? How did doubt manifest itself? What lies have you convinced yourself that it was fine? How long did it take for you to give in to temptation? For instance, it may be that you have purposed not to spend on a month, and you are able to keep that in the first week, but you have this strong desire to buy a smartphone you have been seeing. You don't obtain it in the first week, and you stay committed to what you had purposed. But as days go, doubt starts to rise, your mind starts telling you that if you buy this, it will give you immeasurable benefits and that it remains a viable "investment". You start arguing that not having it is bad and you begin lying to yourself.

Your minds will tell you that since in the last two weeks you didn't spend any money you can now afford this. You start forgetting your bigger plan of saving money and not spending during the month. The temptation is drawing your minds to doubt your decision of "not getting it now". You are tempted to believe it is okay and finally, before the end of the month, you give and buy it. In this time although it took some time, temptation won.

Temptations can also deter us from our goals very easy. For instance, you may bump into your friends in a party and find everyone holding a glass of wine, and you grab the glass and start drinking. In this situation, the thought got into your minds very quickly as you saw the wine. It was easy for you to doubt that this would make a difference in your diet. Your mind will tell you it is only one and then I will stay clear from such for the rest of the day. Sadly, here temptation won in just a few minutes.

Start reviewing your goals and look at what temptations you tend to give in. See whether it relates to people or situations? Is it when you are stressed? Can you visualize your goal? What is pulling you back? Create a journal list concerning it and pay close attention to you and your actions. Know how easily you give in to the four steps. This will be the start to fight your temptation.

Developing Willpower as A Foundation for Success

Willpower can be termed as having the ability to resist short term temptations so that you can achieve your long-term goals. It is the ability to delay your gratification for a specific purpose. Human beings use will power in one way or the other in their everyday life; it may be when resisting the craving to eat sweets or desisting from browsing the internet when there are tasks to be achieved.

It is no doubt that willpower plays an important role in determining whether you will achieve your goals or not. In fact, lack of willpower may be the major hindrance from having good behaviors. Having strong willpower will enable you to achieve more in school, in your career and your personal life.

In life, those people who can delay their gratification have a better chance of having a chance to get into competitive environments and perform better. It is my view that self-discipline and willpower are more important than IQ when one is determined to gain outstanding success.

A very thin line separates success and failure. We can easily succumb to temptation when we are on the verge of succeeding and leave your goal unaccomplished. The presence or lack of willpower will be instrumental in determining if we achieve or fail to attain the set targets. There is a soul in the human body that controls the intellect and mind and gives the mind the ability to overcome the negative characteristics and impulses like inaction, laziness, depression, and procrastination.

People easily become weak in their urge for willpower, and their self-confidence begins to reduce. A great way to improve your willpower is to adhere to a routine of yoga and meditation. During meditation, you will have a state of no-thought that will lead to emptiness which will be instrumental in knowing yourself and discovering the truth. Also, fasting is another way that will help develop willpower. Fasting will not only detoxify the system but will also train you to endure and give you a spirit of self-control and acceptance.

Procrastination

Although it is right to make thoughtful decisions, taking a lot of time to think before getting to a decision can be very bad for any person especially if you are responsible for leadership. When you become too slow to act, react, communicate and make decisions, you are on the verge of failing. Success is always time conscious especially in the current world where there is a lot of competition. People are bound to make decisions swiftly so that they can align themselves to act on what they have purposed.

Whether it is in leadership or in your personal life, you should not take an eternity to decide as this will impact negatively on the outcomes. We all find ourselves procrastinating at a point in our lives and is a mistake that is very easy to make. Failure to make good and swift decisions when we are faced with a crisis can lead to worst consequences.

For everybody, here are some reasons it's important to make decisions quickly:

Time Could Work Against You

It is common for human beings to think that conditions don't change and whatever the decision you must take can wait for some time until you have done all considerations. But that is not always the case only very few things will stay static in this ever-changing world. There are some situations where waiting can work to your advantage. For instance, you may be thinking to fire one of your staffs, -but after taking time without firing him, he decides to resign.

However, many times we will be forced to act very fast and decide rather than waiting for the situation to determine our fate. Making your decision swiftly means that you are in control of what is going around you and within you. Through this, you will be able to take measures that will ensure that you are not caught up amid controversies.

> **When You Fail to Respond You Will Face Huge Problems as Compared If You Had Responded**

Many people learn this the hard way. Some individuals will delay until when people are fed up and have started complaining before taking actions. As a leader, you should not wait until when people have begun holding rallies and demonstrations for you to engage them in communication or handle their grievances. Sometimes it may too late and getting things together again may not be possible.

When you don't procrastinate upon decisions, you will have enough time to do your consultations, and if there is a need for you to apologize, you will do it. You may at times find yourself in a place where your apology will not be taken in good faith because you stayed long before delivering your apology. This might cost you your career or even lose several the closest people in your life.

When You Make Your Decisions Late, You Will Affect People in Ways You Could Not Anticipate

You should not think that you know how people will react when you decide late. People respond differently when subjected to unexpected announcements. For example, when I was at college, the management of the school decided to stop providing our payments towards the expenses on health plan until 5 hours when those plans were to expire. The funny thing is that the university knew that the decision had been overturned more than one month ago but delayed until the last moment to inform us.

You can tell what followed next after this last-minute announcement – the whole institution backfired. We walked out, and the administration was forced to overturn its ruling and eventually paid its share of the health plans through fellowships. If they had told us in advance, they could not have experienced that unfriendly situation, and maybe they could have gotten away with it.

Only A Few Decisions Are Not Reversible
Sometimes a lot of people procrastinate because they think that the kind of decision, they will make is not reversible. However, it is good to understand that most decisions that you can make can be altered later. Most people may see you as a flip-flopper, but by providing a clear explanation of what led you to change your mind is likely to silence your critics. In my opinion, it is much better to flip-flop instead of doing nothing at all.

It Gives You Time to Apologize and Reconcile
When you make timely decisions, and in any case, they cause friction among your colleagues, you will have time to apologize and get everyone on board again. Apologizing is a powerful tool to diffuse even fiercest critics and gain respect from some of them. Therefore, acting on time will not only mean that you will have things done on time but also give you an opportunity to apologize if things go amiss.

Chapter 2:
Self-Discipline Fundamentals

All of us wish to have success in our lives. Maybe you are trying to lose weight or succeed in business. But have you ever asked yourself why achieving weight or succeeding in business or career is not possible for most people? Did you find a convincing reason? If not, stay on because in this chapter we shall help you unravel how commitment and believing in yourself are key fundamental in losing weight and the success of your business.

Most people have attempted to lose weight at a point in their life. Some were not successful because they did not stay committed while others did not believe that their plan was going to work. Others wish that they could become world-class business people but don't start any business, and so their business idea remains just on their minds. Always note that although all things start as an idea in our minds, for you to achieve your set goals, you should be involved and commit yourself to a plan of self-empowerment and have a great conviction that your plan is going to work.

Edgar D. Moranis

The first step towards success in life is staying committed. To better explain this, I will use dieting as an example. Losing weight may seem like a simple thing, but for you to achieve it, you will need to exercise a high level of commitment. Most individuals trying to lose weight are not consistent with the right practices that would help them to lose weight. Most of them usually start well and appear to show results during the first days after they have started. However, very few achieve their long-term goals of losing weight. The reason is that most people do not know the secret of staying committed.

For you to lose a substantial amount of weight in the long-term, you should be able to maintain a certain weight loss for over five years. Always stay committed and engage in high-level physical activities, eat a diet with low calories and maintain a consistent eating pattern all days.

Sometimes after you have just started on your journey to lose weight, you may not realize that you are losing weight. It is normal for you not to see any difference on the scale during the first days or weeks, but this should not make you worried that you aren't losing fat. The bodyweight usually tends to change by only a few pounds. The foods that you take are the primary determinants, and sometimes the hormones can have a big impact on the level of water your body can retain (particularly in women). Therefore, when you don't notice a huge change in your scale don't give up yet but rather stay committed and stay put in your plan.

I Will Teach You to Master Self-Discipline

For you to enjoy a long-term weight loss success, you should experience a maintained weight loss for a duration between two and five years. After this duration, you will have a higher chance of having long term success. During these 2 to 5 years, what happens is that your daily commitment to follow a certain plan each day will transform into long-term self-discipline.

When you are overweight and have decided to lose weight, you should pick the right diet that makes sense to you especially a low-carb diet and stay on it for several months. Learn all the guidelines and follow them. If you take those guidelines seriously, you will be surprised at how much weight you can lose in the long-term, and unlike most first-time dieters, you will achieve your goal right away. Some people tend to try over ten different diets before achieving weight loss but with commitment and believing in your plan, it is possible to hit your target in about three months with trying other diets. Once you change your habits and stick with them, you will be amazed at how easy you can maintain a healthy weight.

Staying committed to your plan means you will carefully keep track of what you are eating. Being cautious of what you are eating and what you should not is very important. You might argue that many individuals who don't lose weight are not careful on the type of food they are eating. But the secret to losing weight is not majorly the type of food that you eat but rather being able to commit to it and believe that it will bring the result you expect. The key to losing and maintaining weight is having the ability to follow a plan and stick to it until you attain your intended goals. When I was 25 years, I was overweight by about 20 pounds. When I decided to cut some weight, I choose a diet that I felt it could help me. I adhered to it for some months, but when I noticed that I was losing some weight, I started changing my diet.

I realized that when I stopped being committed to my plan and started doubting it, I started gaining weight again. Just like most first-time dieters, I did not experience success immediately. I tried various diets and could not achieve my goals. When I talked to my nutritionist, he was shocked to hear that I had changed my diet several times. I was advised on the need of staying committed to my plan and believe that it would work. I stopped returning to my old ways and practices, and I am to say that after I had altered my practices and adhered to them, I was able to maintain a healthy weight.

You can't have that business success that you so much desire without commitment and believing in yourself. Today there is more and more business drafted than before, but do all these proposals see the light of the day? Are you among those individuals that wake every morning and imagine the great opportunities that life has to offer and do nothing? Success in any area of your life and particularly in business is earned and not something you can obtain by wishing only. This reminds me of a common saying that goes " if wishes were horses beggars would ride". Have you ever asked yourself what commitments some of the greatest billionaires in the USA and around the world have made so that they can possess the kind of success they have? Don't worry you will get your answer below.

One crucial thing you should note is that the kind of commitment you have will determine how successful you will become. It is shocking that a lot of individuals usually stop at the "wish" point and don't purpose to endure the struggle and commit to their goals. This is the main reason that makes most people not to succeed. You cannot have a short path to success; you can only attain success through staying committed and believing that your plan is going to work. The path to success is not as smooth as it may look. Otherwise, we would all be successful. You must make a lot of sacrifices so that you can have a life that you have always dreamed of.

Some of the Commitments Essential for Your Success

#1 Commitment: Belief in Yourself

Before other people begin to believe in you, you must believe in yourself. Whatever the dreams you have, be sure to believe in them and trust that you have what it takes to accomplish them. What happens with most people is that they highly underestimate their abilities, and this becomes the main hindrance to discovering their potential.

Note down all your strengths, greatest achievements, uniqueness and accomplishments and remind yourself of them each morning. This can greatly help in strengthening belief in yourself. Most people have much potential, but they are drawn back by having low self-esteem. The important thing is to believe in yourself and your abilities.

#2 Commitment: Acting Massively Daily

After you have decided on what you want to pursue in life, put in place an action plan towards it. Regardless of whether you have set small or huge goals, there is need to commit yourself to act each day massively without excuses.

The first step to involve yourself in towards this is to ensure your minds are prepared to chase your goals passionately. Start by having a plan. While there are many planning tools to assist you in making your plan, be sure to customize your plan to be line with your needs and abilities. Be very realistic while doing this so that you will remain inspired to take the necessary actions each day without fail.

#3 Commitment: Be Adaptive and Learn Always

Being able to adapt and passionate can lead you to greater levels in life. It is surprising that some individuals are so rigid in their minds that they usually reject any suggestions given to them. This can be so detrimental to both their professional and general life.

Charles Darwin said, " It is not the strongest of the species that survives, not even the most intelligent that survives. It is the one that is the most adaptable to change."

Therefore, it is important that you learn from those that you desire as this is something that can impact positively in life. Learn continually without stopping because in many cases there are several ways of handling the same issue. When you change your mind and learn to adapt, you will see more chances in ways that you have never imagined.

#4 Commitment: Be Willing to Lose Sleep and Say NO

People who experience success are those people who are willing to take any step to attain success. You will not only need to work hard, but you will also need to say no to some things that do not go in line with your goals and dreams. It is gratifying and tempting to spend time with your friends for a party or shopping but staying committed on your startup or revising a blog you had written is what would make you experience a real difference. If you are held up in your job during the daytime, the only time you can pursue your own dreams is working during the night, which means thus you will sacrifice some hours of your sleep.

Another way to show commitment in your goals is by saying NO. sometimes it may be challenging to say NO to friends, but by doing so you will start experiencing more success and happiness than other people who have no courage to say NO.

#5 Commitment: Avoid Immoral or Unethical Stuff

You can achieve success through two different ways: an easy way or a difficult way. When you take an easy way, it means that you will do anything to get there – by hook or by crook. This implies that you will take shortcuts, practice unethical things, receiving favors just for the sake of achieving your goal. However, commitment does not involve in any of the above.

It is easy to get seduced to do unethical stuff so that you can have quick results. However, it is good to note that quick results come with a price and can easily ruin you in a short time. Always know that the journey towards success will test your character together with dedication.

#6 Commitment: Proper Work and Life Balance

If you didn't know the most single most important thing in your life is your health. Both your mental and physical health play a significant role in your life because all things are either directly or indirectly dependent on your health.

You should entertain a habit of working hard for so many hours that you forget how important your health is. If for instance, you have worked for 30 good hours, it is good to allow your body rest as it deserves. If working even during the weekends, find a time to relax with people close to you so that you can feel refreshed.

#7 Commitment: Never Give Up

This may sound like a cliché, but ever giving up especially on yourself is the blocker to success. When walking through life, falling is inevitable. There are times when your falling will be due to some of the mistakes you have done, and it is okay. Life has many unexpected occurrences, but you should never allow this to affect your spirit negatively in any manner.

Always be reminded that for you to achieve and tap your best potential, you will need a lot of faith. This spirit will enable you when you are going through tough times. Don't fail to believe that your plan will work.

Commitment means staying loyal to what you said you will do even after the mood that you said it in is gone. Now, it is up to you to decide to stay committed and take actions or let situations control you.

Chapter 3:
Habits of Winners

Self-discipline is at the mind and heart of any successful individual. Whether this is a success in their professional or personal life, it all begins with an inner ability to have self-control though discipline. For you to have that success that you are admiring you must put your minds, emotions, habits, and behaviors under check.

If you in dire need of achieving those great goals that you have set, it is paramount that you understand how self-discipline having is a crucial ingredient to your success journey. The best thing is that self-discipline is not a new thing in the world. In fact, there has been a long-time discussion concerning self-discipline, and it has been exhibited by some of the most successful persons in the world. Our ability to succeed is in any area of our life is majorly dependent on the right habits that we form while still young. However, you cannot achieve those good habits without having the ability to discipline your behaviors and actions. I am a strong believer of the fact that with self-discipline, almost everything is possible. You will be amazed at how much confidence you will gain through being self-disciplined.

I Will Teach You to Master Self-Discipline

Most successful people have attributed their success to self-discipline and believe that self-control is the gateway to achieving any goal in life. For the sake of your success, you must learn how to make use of self-discipline in your life to achieve your goals. Successful people have leveraged on this art of self-discipline through setting a foundational set of good behaviors that allowed to see things the others could not see.

Many may ask how self-discipline is attained or created? What makes one individual have what looks like total control of their actions and habits, while others try but fail? How is it possible for one individual to be very keen on the actions they take every day, while others don't? The answer to these concerns is based on the habits. Since about forty oy your behavior is determined by habit, it is essential to check on your habits for you to attain self-discipline.

Let us look at habits are key to self-discipline. When you practice the below habits, you can have a good foundation within which you can achieve your dreams. Without possessing these habits and actions, it will be like you are chasing the wind which is merely impossible.

Habits: The Foundation to Self-Discipline

Having that what we do most every day is based on our habit, developing the right habit will be instrumental in having the right levels of discipline in our lives. One may be asking, where do habits originate from and through which ways can you achieve them? And what makes us when we strive to alter our habits through either breaking our bad behaviors or exercising the right habits, we are only able to follow that route for a certain period before going back to our former ways?

The greatest challenge, particularly with habits and actions that most people have experienced for a long time is that the minds are used to neural pathways. Neural pathways are required when linking neural networks for a specific function like going up the stairs, smoking, or when preparing something in a certain manner.

Neural pathways allow behavior automation that is repeated constantly with an aim to minimize conscious power of processing in mind. This will, in turn, allow your mind to concentrate on anything else that might be happening. This is built from when we are young and makes part of our genetic makeup and allows the mind to be more efficient so that it can be used in many other things.

However, in most cases, repeated normal behaviors tend to hold us back. In most cases, we have a lot of bad habits that impact negatively on our lives as compared to possessing good habits that could push us forward.

However, instilling the following habits in life, you will discover that achieving the self-discipline will be much easier. Again, you should note that either forming or breaking a habit will take time.

Gratitude

Do you find yourself spending much of your time wishing for things? Then having the habit of gratitude can significantly help you to move from constantly wishing for what you lack and instead appreciate what you have. When you exercise this, you will notice significant shifts beginning to happen. Gratitude has far-reaching impacts. They ranginess from having improved mental health, to your emotional wellbeing, to your spirituality. Gratitude can bring a lot of changes in you, but most importantly it allows you to move from the state of scarcity to a state of abundance.

When you live in a state of lack, it becomes nearly impossible to work on being self-disciplined and attaining your goals. You will spend most of your time worrying concerning what we lack and live in a state of fear, always forgetting what we possess. When you live in a state of lack for long, it can easily lead to physical issues. It may lead to the production of stress hormones like cortisol and epinephrine, which can affect many parts of your body.

As part of promoting self-discipline, spend about 5-10 minutes and see the things you are thankful about. You may see as if there is nothing for you to show gratitude for but search for it.

Meditation

Meditation is key in helping your minds be at peace. It gives you spiritual centeredness that gives room for growth. When you in meditation, you stay clear of all the noise and discover that you are among the beings in the universe that are well connected. Also, meditation is an important key when you are trying to promote self-discipline. It helps clear your mind palette and gives you the best tone for the day. It is instrumental in allowing you to have an improved emotional, mental, spiritual and physical health, allowing you to have huge benefits within a short time.

You don't require much time for you to meditate. You can do it in about ten minutes. You only need to ensure that your minds are quiet and don't allow them to wander. When you notice your mind begins to wander, reel them back. Ensure your energy is grounded in the earth, open your palms while facing the heavens and make sure you are feeling the air when breathing in and out.

Because meditation involves aligning the physical body with your spiritual, it allows you to live a focused life with no worries concerning common issues that usually brings people down. In simple terms, it makes your load light.

Nutrition

Did you know that your body spends about 10-25% of your energy to process and digest food? When you take a diet that is rich in fats, carbohydrates or even proteins, your body will spend a lot of energy in processing that food, and sadly much of those foods will not be helpful to us.

Both raw food and fruits will give the greatest boost for energy as they need less energy during processing and surprisingly will provide more energy for your body to use.

The kind of energy you have within you plays a significant role in determining how focused you will be. When you are focused, you can face your dreams with a lot of discipline. On the other hand, when you are negatively affected by the food that you have taken, it will not be easy to achieve discipline. You will spend a lot of your time feeling sluggish to get anything accomplished.

Therefore, purpose to eat healthy food during breakfast and any other meal of the day. For you to attain this, you must plan on what to eat and restrict yourself from bad habits. Avoid fast foods because they will not give you the energy that your body requires to face your dreams with discipline. Also, food can alter the neurochemical composition of your brain, which has a significant influence on the connection between your body and mind. Go for raw, healthy and organic foods if possible and avoid taking junk foods.

Sleep

Sleep is directly related to your ability to stay disciplined. Getting the right amount of sleep is important to ensuring anything is done. When you don't get enough sleep for a long time, it will affect your mood, your ability to focus, your judgment, your nutrition and your health in general. In fact, when you deprive yourself of sleep for an extended period, things might get out of hand for you as this can cause certain diseases and affect your immune system.

Sleeping for 6-8 hours is important no matter how busy you may be. Also, avoid drinking a lot of caffeinated drinks for a minimum of five hours before you go to bed because caffeine can interfere with your natural sleeping cycle. During the day, it is advisable to avoid too many toxins from cigarettes, alcohol and some medications if possible.

Generally, benefits that come from having enough sleep are more. Despite helping you be more disciplined, you will have improved memory, restrain inflammation and pain, reduce stress, promote your creativity, make your more attentive and limit your chances of being depressed.

Exercise Regularly

Having a habit of exercising regularly is a significant key to self-discipline. It provides a foundation to a life full of good and positive actions, free from wrong habits. Do you really aspire to discipline yourself? Practice the key habit of exercising daily in your mornings. Although benefits that come from exercising regularly are immeasurable, most people have not yet purposed to make exercise a priority in their daily routines.

While most people are running up and down during the day to get things done, they are making a huge mistake by not doing exercises.

Most people argue that they can't be able to put up with this habit or that they have a lot to handle instead of exercising. But that is where they get it wrong.

When you embrace this key of regular exercise, you will not only become more disciplined, but you will also find your life improved in many ways. First, exercising regularly will help minimize the levels of stress and pain when it releases endorphins and neurotransmitters like dopamine and serotonin.

Secondly, exercise regularly will enhance your health by enhancing the flow of blood and increase oxygen in the body cells and ultimately help the body fight diseases and improve your immune system. Again, exercise will help you to remain more focused on a task and enabling you to live a life full of discipline. When instilling the habit of regular exercise in your life, begin small. You can start by having a walk in the morning for five minutes. When you have done that for about a week, you can then increase that to ten or more minutes for another week. As you on with this pattern for more weeks increasing bit by bit, you will realize that you have created a habit without much struggle.

Forgiveness

When most of your days are filled with anger, guilt, and regret, we experience more problems than solutions. In fact, you will need more energy to sustain hate and anger as opposed to when exercising love and forgiveness. When you learn to forgive, you will be able to let some things go. It is hard for you to achieve self-discipline without exercising a habit of forgiveness. This is because most of the time you will be worried about how so and so wronged you that you fail to concentrate on your important goals like achieving self-discipline.

If you have been wronged by a person or a group of people, try and forgive. This does not basically mean that you forget. It only means that you will not unnecessary energy holding grudges. When you forgive, you are letting go of the negativity that deters from achieving self-discipline--trying to discipline yourself? Forgiveness gives you a major avenue. Although it may not initially appear like a habit of discipline, it remains among the most significant ones.

I cannot promise you that it is easy to forgive but looking at the benefits that you will benefit personally after you have forgiven, it is worth doing it. Think about all the people that have longed you and find a reason to forgive. One of the ways to forgive them is to put yourself in their place and think if you could have done differently if you were in their situation. Look for humor and find a lesson that you learned from what happened.

It is until you let go of those bad feelings towards other people that most things in your life will start improving. Restrain yourself from being worried and being stressed so that you can move forward towards self-discipline.

Be Organized

I Will Teach You to Master Self-Discipline

For you to attain self-disciplined and succeed in your dreams, you must be organized. Being organized is a habit that you need to fully incorporate no just in your professional life but also in your personal life. This means that you must keep both your home and office organized in line with things in your minds. You can't have an organized life minus discipline – they are intertwined. If you are disorganized, you will need to start small as you improve each day. You can organize one small space in the kitchen on the first day, while the following day you move to organize your bedroom.

Just like any other habit, you will need patience so that the habit of organization can be built. You will need to put some effort and be attentive, but after some time, you will see the benefits. When you have organized the physical space surrounding you, your mind will relax, stress will reduce, and you will be more focused.

Ultimately, it is easy to gain more self-discipline when you have an organized life. This entails that you will put anything in its right place when you are through using it. It's the small things that you do each day that largely impacts on the kind of life that you live. Always be attentive to small things in life, and you will benefit largely.

Persistence

My list of habits that are key for self-discipline would be incomplete without persistence. Persistence is needed if you are to go through tough situations and not give up. It also helps you in the case that you fail or fall you get back to your feet and push forward. Without being persistent, it would be almost impossible to achieve self-discipline. The reason I say this is because achieving your goals is not easy. It is easy to get discouraged and give up that staying put and pushing forward particularly if by pushing forward you are experiencing pain or discomfort.

The point to take note of here is that even the most successful individuals that we admire and see them as role models have gone through failure multiple times. Failure is important in pushing our determination forward, and without it, we could not achieve some of the goals that we put in place.

Chapter 4:
Millionaire Self-Discipline Secrets

Sometimes back I was experimenting a crazy diet where I fasted for 18 hours and only ate the food that I admired for the six hours. I was introduced to this diet by one of my workout partners and what I realized while I was on this plan is that I had unusual urge to take snacks at midnight or a meal at around three in the morning. It was a challenge to stay without having a bite from my hidden packet of chips. I know this is a common battle to you too, where you find yourself fighting with your inner critic where you have one side arguing it is okay to give in to the wrong side whereas the other try to convince you not to break the promise or target you set for yourself. Many times, you may find yourself experiencing struggles that lead to a major conflict in your minds. You may be struggling to lose weight, but you have the unfortunate urge pushing you away from exercising. You don't know how valuable your couch is to you until you start having the idea to work out.

The reason you find self-discipline, so challenging is because it demands your conscious to act in a certain manner regardless of what your emotions are. It is common when waking up in the morning for your emotions to try and convince you to stay in the best and snooze the alarm. But you must apply your conscious minds that tell that it is wrong to miss work or school that will enable you to move out of your comfort zone. This happens to me frequently, especially on Mondays. I am always tempted to snooze the alarm and go back to sleep instead of going to work. Was it not for my conscious telling me that my boss will not tolerate me missing for work; I could easily give in.?

I know you are asking yourself, why is it too hard to have self-discipline throughout when we are trying to accomplish our goals? Why are we not able to follow to the goals that we set our minds onto daily? Most challenges that people face are as a result of our failure to maintain self-discipline. From harmful addictions, overeating, debts, and laziness have greatly impacted negatively to our economy.

In your day to day activities, you use willpower, either knowingly or unknowingly. The mistake that is common to most people is that when they hear about self-discipline, they think that it only applies to major tasks that they have yet to do. However, you need to apply self-discipline even in smaller tasks like refusing the temptation to eat a donut in the morning. You use willpower when you decide not to get upset after you are caught in a snarl-up on your way to work or even you when you decide not to fight a person who embarrasses you. Without much ado, look at the below mind tricks that will help you master self-discipline:

Eat More Often

I know this may sound weird, but it is one of the tricks you can use to master your discipline. Your brain is a power-plant that requires regular replenishment. Individuals that always starve themselves have shown to have low self-discipline as compared to those who eat regularly. However, this does not necessarily mean that you should be overeating as that would lead to the development of unnatural bad habits. This means that your body requires a steady glucose level which helps give energy to the brains and other vital body organs.

In simple terms, glucose acts as fuel to your brains so that they can work perfectly. When you have a low level of glucose in your blood, you are prone to making poor judgments that may lead to regrets in the coming days. Therefore, it is good to begin your day with a healthy breakfast or eat a light meal before undergoing a test. If you experience instances when you feel irritated, take something small. On my case, having fruits, a light meal or even a drink saves me a great deal.

The only caution you should take when eating is to avoid taking unhealthy foods. Sometimes you may even be forced to stay away from environments where such foods are found.

Handle One Goal at a Time

What has made a lot of people fail to accomplish their goals is handling so many tasks at a go. This makes it hard for them to stay committed in any of them. This is the same mistake people make when setting up the New Year's resolutions. Sometimes you may start a project out of excitement, but as time goes, you may realize that you put yourself in so much work. It may make you get worn out and drained, and you may find yourself losing interest on the project as you had before.

To ensure you have maintained self-discipline in your mind, ensure you work on each goal at a given time. This will enable you to maintain your willpower more easily because you will not be overwhelmed with so many tasks that would add up on the way.

Have A Strong Believe About Willpower

A person's willpower is directly proportional to their beliefs. This means if an individual had low-level willpower, they would be met by limited possibilities. On the other hand, if a person had strong willpower, it will not be easy to get exhausted before achieving their goals. Although there are still ongoing engagements among scientists concerning the willpower, a lot of suggestions are showing that the concept you have towards willpower will come true.

When you have a limited belief, you are always going to experience obstacles on your way which will be your limitations. Before realizing it, you will have already set your mind to fail. This means that for you to succeed, you will require a huge boost in motivation.

Use Rewards

I Will Teach You to Master Self-Discipline

Our minds work in a way that they work towards something. When you set rewards for yourself when you achieve something, you will be motivated to work much harder towards achieving it. You may be arguing, but I have huge aspirations, do I still to motivate myself through rewards? Yes, because in some cases you may feel like what you are doing is not worth and therefore using rewards means you will see what you are doing is worth doing.

You can set yourself mind in a way that you will only get a certain reward after you are through with a task. This will help you reinforce yourself and become a more disciplined person.

Put in Place Alternatives or Backup Plan

This means taking situations that you usually face and have an alternative way out of it. For example, let's say you are working towards eating healthy, and you find yourself in a party with your buddies. You should have an answer to let's say a person offers you fatty foods. You should deny it and instead ask for your favorite drink instead or even water. This will allow you to have a self-intended mindset instead of jumping into situations blindly. This will prevent you from making wrong choices based on majority or the state of your emotions.

No one knows you like yourself in the world. You know your strengths and your habits. So, for you to ensure you don't fall on bad traits, have an alternative way to get out of it. Remind yourself how you would act if you knew the obstacles heading your way. If you know it's hard for you to exercise when you arrive home, have a plan to do nothing else when you get home before doing your exercises. When you have a plan for you to follow, there are higher chances that you will achieve it.

Don't Allow Yourself to Be Distracted

Out of sight out of mind rule will significantly help here. This is a powerful way to master your self-discipline by avoiding temptations that can disembark you from your goals. When you are constantly surrounded by things that cause you temptation, it will lead to unnecessary battles in the minds. Sometimes you may find yourself battling whether you should take candy in the bowl resting on the table or not. When you experience these hard decisions, your skills for making decisions and energy will be drained. This energy is required for you to make good decisions.

If you know you have other things to deal with in the house, avoid unnecessary temptations like the internet and television. An effective way to avoid internet is to stay away from major social networks and continue with your work. Through this, you will have strong willpower to do your assignments with little or no interruptions at all.

Assess Your Ability to Withstand Pain

The foundation of self-discipline lies in having the ability to overcome pain. Know how much suffering you are willing to take in order to achieve your goals. Always note that not everything is worth suffering for, and not every suffering produces results. Begin the day by asking yourself ``what suffering am I willing to go through today?" be honest to yourself because we all have a limit to our pain tolerance. Being honest will enable you to find ways to achieve goals that are in line with your limits.

Most people fail because they make the mistake of overestimating their limits. What this means is that when they are subjected to difficult situations, they will find it hard to withstand until they can achieve their goals.

Ensure Consistency

If you are the kind of person who makes excuses on almost everything you will neither attain self-discipline nor be happy. You must not allow yourself to make excuses concerning your kids or lack of time. Always find time for what is important to you. Be it is daily on monthly start small and keep going. Commit yourself no matter how hard and rough it may seem.

If you have purposed to go to the gym for the purpose of losing weight, don't allow anything to push you back. Perform your exercises daily. You can start with a ten minutes' walk during the first week as you increase by 5 minutes each week. Through this you will remain consistent and achieving your goal will be easy. You cannot achieve self-discipline without consistency.

Employ Muscle-Building Skills in Decision Making

Building self-discipline works the same way as heading to the gym to build muscles. This means that the more you practice it, the firm it becomes. A good starting place is to visualize how perfect you will get things done, imagine and have a mental picture of the advantages and satisfaction you will have once you have accomplished them. When you have a clear vision of your goal in your head, you will be motivated.

Monitoring Your Progress

After you have in place a clear goal, a better way to ensure you remain committed is to monitor your progress frequently. Some individuals will not, however, require a tracker because they spent a very long-time mastering both their willingness and self-discipline. However, for those starting, it is important to keep track of each step they are making towards their goals because of failure to that they may give up and ultimately forget.

When you have a journal of your actions, you will realize that tracking your work will help you how much you have accomplished. This will make you proud when you discover what you have achieved by the end of the day. Although you may not have attained your dreams, you will see how close you are each day.

Chapter 5:
The Fool Proof Method to Achieve Your Goals

Self-control, also called self-discipline is an essential life skill to possess. It is self-control that will enable you to overcome tempting situations in your life and help you to remain on the right path when you are faced with a tough situation. Without self-control, it is hard even to achieve even the easiest task. This is because self-control is instrumental in keeping you composed and work towards your goal. It is self-control that will help you remain focused and not wander and be caught in the confusion that would arise when you follow people blindly.

Having self-control means that you are in control of your emotions and likings, particularly when you are faced with a tough situation. It is the ability to overcome your impulses for the sake of achieving your long-term goals. This implies that you will not be controlled by immediate impulses, but you will take charge of your emotions and avoid doing things that might bring regret in the future. For example, you could have purposed to eat healthily, but are tempted to have that delicious chocolate. If you don't have self-control, you will give in to temptation and take that chocolate and eventually ruin your goal of eating healthy.

Practicing self-control and willpower in difficult situations will cause you to experience great success and achievements in the long run.

Lack of self-discipline can lead to lifelong and life-damaging effects. Man is different from animals because he can impart some degrees of restraint when interacting with fellow humans. If you fail to exercise self-discipline, there might not be a difference between you and the beast. For instance, when a leopard is out there hunting, either he will be successful or not, he has no consideration for the prey, nor does it feel remorse afterward.

Human beings are made in a way that they must live on the framework set up by society. They must coexist with each other. Therefore, it is important for every person to exercise restraint dealings with others. For you to live in a congenial environment, it is necessary to control your actions towards others. However, when you lack control of yourself, there will emerge friction that would arise especially because people possess different personalities and wishes in life. When you deliberately do wrong acts towards others, you are not different from a beast. The idea of self-discipline should be brought out to depict from temptations that would lead to adverse consequences.

For you to have a more structured life and joyful life, you need to have self-control. Imagine what the world would be if every person gave in to his desires and emotions. People will not have control over any aspect of their life.

Self-control is an essential aspect of your personal growth. When you were a baby, you knew very little, but as you grow up, you become cleverer in that more was learned, although you didn't know the difference between good and wrong. However, when you were no longer a toddler, and growing up you know what is right and left through self-control. Therefore, a person can gain self-control as he matures and through exercising discipline and ensuring your emotions are in check.

Self-control is essential in all areas of your life. Be it in your relationships, while at school, in your career or while enjoying yourself with your peers. Having the ability to control yourself is probably the most important trait you will ever possess. Self-discipline is important in promoting patience within yourself. Through self-control, you can restrain some actions and ultimately increasing your ability to tolerate tough or unpleasant situations. You will experience moments of self-control when you get a hold of your emotions and try to make a change in your emotions, to positive.

When you exercise self-control, you will have increased self-esteem, and other people will see you as a person who is disciplined and in full control of your emotions and actions. The funny thing with humans is that it is easy to be controlled by others as compared to having self-control because self-control requires a lot of determination.

We have all seen what self-control is and some of its benefits, but how do we master it? Have a look below:

Methods to Master Self-Control
Having known how important self-control is in your life, it would be better to learn some of the methods you can use to master self-control. Read on and get enlightened.

Have Ways to Manage Stress
Nothing is overwhelming like going through episodes of stress. Therefore, learning how to control and manage stress will save a great deal. You can stop and take a few deep breaths to help slow your heart rate as this will put you in a relaxation mood easily. Be sure to do exercises always, take a healthy diet and have enough sleep. This will help you improve focus and your health in general. When you are experiencing low blood sugar, and you don't have enough sleep, you are likely to make poor decisions. Having regular exercises will enable you to have enough sleep and enables you to have discipline in your diet.

When you have healthy ways to manage stress, you will have enough energy to continue working, and life can feel fulfilling.

Exercise Meditation

Did you know that you can meditate your way to more self-control? When you meditate, you will have self-control skills in various areas that include the management of stress, attention, focus, and impulse control. Those people who have a tendency of meditating regularly, which develops strong willpower.

Stay Healthy

It is easy to give in to temptations when at your weakest point than when you are strong and healthy. When you are unhealthy, it may be easy for your minds to lack self-control. For instance, it may be hard for you to go to the gym and do workouts when you are having bad health. You can attain good health by eating healthy and exercising regularly. When you are unwell, the body will react in negative ways because your reserves are drained and there is not enough energy for the brain. Most arguments at home and any other places happen when people are either tired or hungry. It is easy to know someone who did not sleep enough during the night by looking at how they behave in the morning. A person who did not sleep enough will be easily upset while the one who rested well during the night will be happy and jovial.

Therefore, eating healthy and having enough sleep is essential in ensuring you have a healthy life and eventually a more controlled life.

Avoid Temptations

Human beings are not automatically wired to resist temptation. Most people resist temptation by avoiding it. Training yourself self-control by practicing repeatedly may not automatically lead to improved self-control generally. Therefore, there is no need to beat yourself up when you don't have self-control because we are not automatically wired to it. If we are not wired to self-control, how come we have disciplined people? Most people attain self-discipline by avoiding temptation, and through this, they build self-control effortlessly. You should not struggle to resist temptation but rather avoid/remove temptation.

Set yourself for growth by controlling yourself and what surrounds you by avoiding temptations. This will help you to easily make decisions automatically and reinforce yourself so that you can prioritize the decisions that are more important to you.

Avoid Self-Criticism

Having a habit of self-criticism affects self-control negatively. When you view your setbacks as an indication that you are hopeless will mess a lot of things. This is because your primary goal will be to soothe yourself instead of learning from your experiences. This might, unfortunately, lead to bad habits such as drinking alcohol, eating junk food and being addicted to the internet.

I Will Teach You to Master Self-Discipline

If you find yourself criticizing yourself, exercise self-acceptance instead. This will help you be more compassionate and more productive in achieving what you have purposed to do.

Chapter 6:
How to Break Bad Habits (The Right Way)

Change of any kind is very hard for us to accept and embrace. This is because we are creatures of habit. Most of our day to day activities can be categorized into several replicable habits, that we have developed through genetic predisposition and prior experience combination.

Most of our habits are harmless and are designed to enable us to become more efficient and exist comfortably in society. This includes things like going to the gym, brushing our teeth or browsing through social media regularly so that we can stay up to date. However, some psychologically complex habits are designed to protect we, like when dealing with traumatic situations through humor, staying away from a strong romantic relationship to avoid going through hurt and staying in the same unfulfilling job instead of taking responsibility and take risks.

When we maintain these habits to protect ourselves from failure, discomfort or pain, there is something wrong. Although these habits serve a role in our lives by helping you stay grounded when faced with moments of uncertainty, however over time, they impede mental anxiety and prevent growth. Your thoughts do not only affect your emotions, but they also influence the way you behave. When you have positive thoughts, you will feel better, and your performance will be awesome. On the other hand, when you think negative, you will feel despair, and this will affect your feelings and behavior.

It is normal for you to experience unrealistic, unhelpful and exaggerated negative thoughts at a time in life. When you allow cynicism to become your habit, it will limit your capabilities. It doesn't matter how experienced or talented you are; if you can't control your minds, it will be impossible to achieve great things.

Therefore, the sports psychologists help people looking towards being Olympians and athletes to eliminate the harmful self-talk that would otherwise interfere with their performance. However, not only athletes can experience benefit when they change their mindset, you can as well reap benefits when you start thinking positively. When you discover the habits that deny you of your mental capabilities is the first step towards healing your mindset. Below are some of the bad habits that can sabotage your growth:

Making Excuses
I usually tell my team that the moment you start making excuses is the moment you start failing. Blaming other individuals or circumstances for your lack of success or as the reasoning for your bad

behavior derails your personal growth. Do you find yourself uttering things like," My job is weighing me down," or " All this paperwork is making it hard for me to properly do my work"? - This will impact on your performance. Refrain from a habit of making excuses and focus on things that are strongest instead of the things that you are weak. When you focus on what is positive, it will be easier for you concentrate towards achieving your goals.

You Have Negative Predictions

When you predict negatively about your future, you may just get negative results. If you go to the stage to make a performance with thoughts that you are going to mess up everything, you will not have a good focus, and you may end up forgetting your performance. Our minds tend to do what we tell them to do so being positive might make your minds sharper and free from distractions.

Seeking Approval

You should not make it your primary goal to seek approval from others because sometimes you may get discouraged. When you focus on the other person's approval, you might get in your way of doing better. For instance, let's say you are headed for an interview and in your mind, you are mostly thinking about how the interviewer would perceive your answers. This could mess you up and could make you stumble over words during the interview. Although it is important to gauge your audience's reaction towards your presentation, don't take a lot of time thinking about how they would react, but instead, focus more on your presentation.

Having Self-Doubt
One major thing that can kill your dreams is insecurity. If you walk to the gym thinking that it is impossible to gain muscles or lose weight, it is likely that you will give up before attaining your goals. When you have self-rejection, it will be hard for you to put the required effort towards achieving your goals.

Putting Yourself Down or Despising Yourself
It is difficult to gain self-discipline in any area of your life when you are telling yourself the opposite of what you want to achieve. When I was starting exercises, I could always see myself as a weak person who could not achieve building any muscles. What could happen is I was not zealous about my bodybuilding because I was always putting myself down. Until when I changed that perception about myself, that is when I started achieving my goals.

Second-Guessing Your Choices
Although sometimes it may appear okay to reflect on your past in order to make a more informed decision, second-guessing on every choice you have made could ruin your performance. When you make choices believe in them and put all the effort towards realizing them. When you start doubting, you will not have the courage to fight any challenges that you would face in the process.

Strategies on How to Break from Bad Habits

Bad habits are practices that deter you from attaining your long-term goals. It can be that you have been a chain smoker, or you are addicted to the screen most of the day that you have no time to work on your goals. To break from bad habits is not easy, especially if they bring some enjoyment to you. Below are some of the strategies to break bad habits:

Have A Reason Why You Want to Break from That Habit

For you to succeed in breaking a habit, it is paramount that you have a strong reason as to why you want to break from that habit. Note down all the reason. This will help you feel motivated. Note the harmful effects that you will experience when you continue holding to your bad behavior. For instance, if you have been too lazy to go to the gym, remind yourself of the importance of going to the gym and do workouts. Also, remind yourself what you will lose if you continue sitting on your couch and not exercising. Look at the effects of obesity on your health and how it affects your daily life. Through this, you will be having the motivation required to break from that harmful habit.

Find A Replacement with What You Want Rather

Our brains cannot remain a vacuum. If you want to be free from a bad habit, you need to give your brains a new way to move to. Set a new direction for your brains. For instance, if you want to break from screen addiction, you can use that time when you used to watch with exercise, reading or meditation. You can also minimize your free time by working more on that project you are dreaming of.

Don't Depend on Willpower

Let's be practical here.

Breaking bad habits is difficult, and willpower seems to get on the way for most people. Willpower determines whether you will push through to success or go back to your old habits. So, the secret here is to avoid willpower as you possibly can.

There is an intriguing urge to go back to our old ways on every decision we have purposed to take, and when we try to flex our willpower our "willpower tank" is drained. When the willpower is drained, you have nothing left, and you may be vulnerable to fall back to your former habits.

The secret is avoiding that difficult decision by creating a new habit. For instance, maybe you have decided to wake up early and start working. Knowing how hard it is to wake up at 4:00 a.m., you may need to make the following steps:

- Go to bed earlier

- Put your alarm out of reach while on the bed so that for you to snooze the alarm or switch it off, you will need to wake up

- Choose the clothes you will wear the night before

- Pack water or anything you may need the night before and put them a place where you can easily access them in the morning.

Although there is still some willpower involved, having avoided your willpower to make certain decisions, would help you to be successful.

Analyze the Habit

One of the ways to defeat an enemy is by knowing the tricks and his action plan. When it comes to getting rid of your bad habit, it is no different. Know where, when, why and how you are most affected by your habit. How often do you engage in it? It is paramount to understand your behavior if you desire to alter it. You can make a journal of your habits for a week or a specific duration of time. Study the patterns as this will provide the foundation upon which to change your habits.

Have A Plan and Execute Your Progress

Once you have identified the habit that you want to break, find and focus on the solution. Visualize how success is all about and how you will reach there. Going out for bigger goals might work for some people but starting small and going bit by bit towards achieving your bigger goal might be the best approach. No matter what your determination is, set a timeframe as your goal for when you ought to have completely got free from that habit. Divide your goals into milestones and track your progress as you move forward.

Employ Consistency

I Will Teach You to Master Self-Discipline

A substantial time is required for any habit to have roots in us and solidify in our brains, and so getting rid of it from our brains and learn other habits will also require time. The trick is to remain exercising your new habit. The more you exercise the new habit; it will make it easier for your brain to get used to it. Your brain will lay a foundation upon which you will develop your new habit fully.

For instance, when you are aiming at losing 15 pounds, you will need to go to the gym 4-5 times a week instead of exercising once per week. You will need to embrace consistency because your minds need to adopt and align towards your new direction.

Stop Exercising Bad Habits

Once you have identified a bad habit that is ruining your success and achievements, you should stop doing it. Anything that is not helping you towards realizing your goals should be starved. For instance, once you know that bad company is holding you back from breaking the habit of smoking, you should dissociate yourself from them. Once you have disconnected yourself from bad company, you will find it easy to break bad habits.

Chapter 7:
How to Force Productivity Out of Yourself

Is laziness preventing you from achieving your dreams? Do you have the feeling that your laziness is slowly destroying your life? This is like having a bloodsucking leech that secretly feeds on your leg. Life may seem okay but until you realize that you this parasite feeding you off your progress. For some people, even after realizing that laziness is getting their best of them, they don't do anything to change that. They only shrug their shoulders and allow this "parasite" to continue impacting on their life, progress, and goals. They think that they have a lot of time to change their situation, but what they miss to know is that any moment that goes is an opportunity lost. An opportunity to get rid of laziness and gives themselves a second chance for redemption.

When you choose to walk the path of laziness, you are choosing the easy path where there is no resistance. It is true that the path will bring you pleasure, but that relaxation is both futile and short-lived. In the end, the pleasure will transform into horrible pain the moment you discover that you have ruined your life. The pleasure that seems so good for a short time will turn into lifelong regrets when you realize that you lack enough time or ability to achieve your most desired goals. And as simple as that, once a promising life, turns into a life of suffering and regrets.

What is Laziness?

Laziness is a habit learned over time where we persistently and consistently resist effort in preference of a strong desire to be idle. It is a passive habit and state-of-mind we are not attentive both in our physical and mental. Some things need to be done, but we not be motivated to get them done. Therefore, we don't take proactive steps towards the direction of our goals but rather choose an easy path, where the pleasure we shall have now exceeds the benefits we may wish to get in the future. To better understand laziness, let us look if the difference between procrastination and laziness?

Having said that laziness is as a result of passive behavior, where we tend to resist effort. Procrastination is a bit different in that it is not passive but instead hesitant. This is a reluctant habit that we use to avoid acting. Procrastination is a way of defense against difficulties, potential failure, obstacles, setbacks, and criticism. When procrastinating, we are bound to have guilt. This is because we are willing to act, but we hesitate, and ultimately, we feel miserable.

On the other hand, laziness is not always attached to guilt. It is a careless behavior where one finds comfort in not doing nothing. One is not bothered to act on something strenuous or hard or can't afford to exhaust mental energies on a given task. It becomes easier to indulge in the short-lived pleasure instead of enduring pain while doing something beneficial.

Why Do You Succumb to Laziness?

We all at times succumb to laziness. However, for some people laziness is not a one-time occurrence; it is their everyday behavior. It is a regular behavior that lures us into a false sense of comfort. It may seem sometimes easy to give in to laziness, but when you look at its effects, in the long run, you better desist from it.

There are several reasons that could be making you succumb to laziness. Maybe you are feeling tired, and you use that as an escape so that you can recharge. It may seem okay because our bodies need rest but remember not to confuse rest and laziness. We take rest so that we can recuperate in doing work and putting our effort towards a task while being lazy, we simply ignore a task and use laziness to ignorance.

When you are tired and are feeling somehow bored or uninspired, it may be that you need mental awakening to remain focused and motivated. You can try challenging yourself using new ways or have creative ways to inspire yourself to get going.

You can also become a victim of laziness when you are overwhelmed. In this case, laziness is acting as a defensive mechanism the same way procrastination does. However, here you don't care. You are at a point where you care less about the outcomes, and laziness seems to be the best alternative.

It may also be that you are lazy because you are experiencing hurt or worried to face a situation or something. When you reach a point where you don't give a damn, you choose to involve yourself in laziness without feeling guilt or experiencing shame.

For you to experience the success that you so much desire, you must resist the urge to be lazy. Have a look at the following strategies that will help you defeat laziness:

How to Progress Your Goals or Life When You're Lazy and Not Be Motivated?

If you have reached a point where you are fed up with laziness, and are in search for ways to change, pay much attention to this section. You are losing out on many good things by continuing being lazy. Read on and get enlightened with the following steps:

Step 1: Find the Reason You Are Always Lazy

Like in any other solution finding venture, your first step should be to find the reason you are falling victim for laziness. Pause for a moment and look at all the reasons that make you lazy. You can do this by asking yourself the following questions:

- What is the exact reason that makes you embrace laziness?

- Are you simply uninspired, bored, just overwhelmed or fatigued?

- What are afraid of or avoiding?

- Are you afraid to act or you're using laziness as an avoidance mechanism?

When you understand why you are lazy will help you a lot in building an action plan to overcome laziness. For example, if your laziness is a result of being bored, you will find ways to restrict yourself from being bored. If it is out of fear that you become lazy, you must find better ways to understand your fears.

Step 2: Explore the Long-Term Effects of Laziness

Now that you have discovered the reasons that make you lazy, now it is time to explore the long-term effects of your laziness. You have already seen how laziness lures you with the short-term benefits and pleasures which is well and good. We all fall victim of this sometimes; however, in the long-run, that short-term pleasure may lead to a lot of pain when we start regretting on the opportunities that we missed.

The main reason we find ourselves "finding refuge" in laziness is that there is the absence of enough urgency or pain to make us do the opposite. We have a short-term view of life and base our decisions on what will make you feel good now. And in such situations, laziness presents itself as the best alternative. It provides us with short moments of pleasure without experiencing guilt or pain.

Therefore, for you to break the cycle of laziness, try and refocus yourself. You must shift on your focus and attention. This means that instead of concentrating on the short-term pleasure that comes with laziness, you should focus on the long-term effects that will come if you continue to fall victim of laziness. Laziness eats us slowly by slowly as time goes by and its consequences may not be seen now, but in the long run, its effects will be far-reaching.

When you are tempted to give in to laziness, ask yourself:

- How does laziness hurt you?

- What are you potentially missing as a result of laziness?

- What are the long-term results if you continue giving in to laziness?

When you regularly give in to laziness, you are strengthening it. Sadly, laziness will lead to negative consequences due to missed opportunities.

Step 3: Put in Place Achievable and Challenging Targets

One mistake that people make when setting goals is to set goals that are so much beyond their abilities. When they are overwhelmed by those goals, they might use laziness as an escape mechanism. Therefore, when setting your goals, make sure they are achievable but at the same time challenging. Keep them challenging enough to maintain your stimulation and interest. Pursuing a much easier goal can also lead to boredom, which is a major trigger of laziness. People who embrace a habit of laziness have no clear and concise goals. And for the few who have, they are not inspired by their goals to wake up in the morning with passion and energy.

The secret to getting rid of laziness is to have a clear picture of what you are looking for. Asking yourself the following questions might help:

- What do you dream of achieving?
- What goals stimulates or inspires you daily?
- What projects are passionate about?
- Why are you achieving those goals?
- What goals are achievable but challenging?
- Why must you achieve these goals?

Asking yourself these questions will help you in setting your goals. However, this is not enough. A lot of people set goals and do nothing towards achieving them. For you not to fall into this class, you must be specific on what is required to achieve those goals. You should know what is exactly involved in making your goals achievable. Know the routines you will need to develop and act as a foundation to attain your goals and know major tasks you would need to employ for you to hit your target.

After you have identified what is needed to achieve your goals, create stimulating tasks that offer both the challenge and excitement to you. If you set boring tasks, it is easier for you to go back to your lazy ways. Have a specific deadline within which you should achieve your tasks as this will encourage you to work more quickly. However, note that setting deadlines and priorities alone will not help you to overcome laziness completely. Ensure your tasks are engaging, fun and enjoyable.

Step 4: Take Quick Small Actions

When trying to overcome laziness, don't make the mistake of doing too much in a short period. This will cause you to be overwhelmed.

It is true that after you have laid out your goals and outlined the tasks to focus on, you may find it necessary to take immediate actions without delay. However, be sure to do this by taking small actionable steps. Concentrate on one thing at a time. Through this, you will avoid the pressure that would come in trying to achieve all your goals once but do things at the pace you are comfortable.

Ask yourself:

- What is that one thing you could do that would take you closer to your goal?

- What should you focus on primarily?

While working on your task, remind yourself:

- Making a few steps is better than not making any step at all

- After the pain you are experiencing now, you will have the pleasure

- You'll do what is necessary now for you to have what you want later

Remember even in the long-distance race; the slow and steady emerges the winner. Don't put yourself in the pressure of trying to do everything at a go. Just do something and do it consistently over time and you will see the progress. For instance, if you are targeting losing 20 pounds in your weight, don't beat yourself up when you don't realize it within one week. Have a plan and execute it consistently and before you know it, you will realize your goal. That's the only way you can achieve your goal and be happy.

Chapter 8:
The Morning Routine Fix

There is a saying that goes, "the early bird catches the worm". Have ever thought what walking up would mean for your career, your business or studies? It can bring a lot of impacts if incorporated with the right mindset. What I have learned over time is that you no need to set your alarm to wake you up very early in the morning if you are going to sit on your screen before starting your work. Having a good morning routine is about having the right mindset and doing the important things first before anybody takes your attention.

Maybe you are the kind of person who is always obligated and have so much to handle that you feel you are always running short of time. You can change all that and have a productive and organized day by exercising a good morning routine. Most successful people use morning routines as a deal breaker towards a successful and productive day.

Having a great morning routine does not revolve about who achieves more than the other; it is about giving yourself an opportunity to start the day with peace, confidence, and positivity. Starting your day well will enable you to complete your tasks as expected and deal with whatever comes your way without much pressure or stress.

Why is Having a Morning Routine Important?

Helps You Become More Productive

When you have a morning routine, it will help you tone for your day. It gives the ability to take charge of your schedules instead of schedules taking charge over you. When you begin your day well, you will be more focused on what is ahead, and manage your time well, and ultimately your productivity will increase.

Being productive does not only revolve around how much you have achieved but also the quality of willingness you are putting towards your tasks. For instance, you can end the day with eight attempted but not completed tasks, and another person does only four but fully completed tasks. The one with four fully completed tasks will feel proud than you because of the quality of work he has done. Having a well functional morning routine will mean that you will find a well-planned day minus stress.

You Will Have Both Emotional and Physical Health

It is evident that when you begin your day right by having a great morning routine, the remaining part of your day will be stress-free. You will not have pressure when in your working place which is common among most working people. When you minimize stress will be compromised, and you will be safe from diseases such as allergies, flu, colds, and other common health problems.

Again, your emotional is mostly dependent on your physical health. Again, it is hard to remain smiling when you have been caught up by tasks that need to be done. When you are late you will be overwhelmed and even frustrated. When this becomes the order of the day, you will feel like giving up because you may think it is impossible to get on track again. To avoid this, have a morning routine as it will be instrumental in giving both physical and emotional health.

You Will Be More Confident
When you go through the day completing all the tasks that you had purposed, your confidence will be boosted. Morning routine gives you confidence in that it helps you to prioritize things, manage your time and be more productive.

You Will at Peace
Imagine what goes through your mind when you see yourself as a failure each day. It can cause a lot of damage to your relationships, careers, emotions and your physical. You will always experience negative voices that will lead to distress and feel overwhelmed. You can save yourself from this by having a good morning routine that you are consistent with. It will allow you to exercise meditation, which will give you a significant way to begin your day. When you organize your day and be successful, you will be more peaceful knowing that you

have achieved your day's goals. When you become consistent in fulfilling your day's tasks, your life will be peaceful generally.

For you to have a fruitful day, you must exercise some right habits.

Below is a six-morning ritual that most successful people have adopted and seen results, although they may seem difficult to practice.

Make Your Plan the Yester Night

Although this is not a morning routine, it is a habit that will play a significant role in having a fruitful morning routine. Therefore, for you to have a productive morning, have put in place plans the night before your morning. Having your things for the following day set before the morning comes is much more helpful in achieving your goals. Buy anything you feel you will need for your breakfast and write down a schedule on what you need to be accomplished the following day.

All these may sound very easy for you but believe me that by the time you arrive home after the day's work, the last thing your minds would like to think is about tomorrow's plans. You are easily tempted to get in your couch and enjoy your favorite drink, thinking that tomorrow will worry for itself.

Embrace A Habit of Waking Very Early

If you are like me, I like snoozing my alarm anytime I don't feel like waking up, but for the sake of having a successful morning, you should let this habit go. For the past two to three years I have been studying about morning routines, I have been able to learn that the most successful people wake before 6 a.m. and others even before 5am during weekdays.

I know this does not sound well to most of us, but considering the benefits that you will get, it's worth the sacrifice. The point to go with here is: successful mornings begin very early in the morning.

Begin the Day with Exercises

Although only a few people want to wake up and do exercises in the morning, it has many good things. Morning is likely the best moment to do your workouts. When you begin the day with exercise, it will not be easy for you to put it off. I came to see morning exercises as an important component of our life when I realized that even the busiest people in the world find time to exercise in the morning. I came to think if some of the prominent CEOs can find time for this what of me? A good example is the former president of USA Barack Obama, begins his day with early exercises. Despite him being too busy than most of us, he finds time to exercise. I concluded it must be a very important habit to include in our daily lives.

Handle Your Most Important Projects

I usually use my morning hours to handle some of my high-priority work because at that time there are few interruptions. It also allows me to give it more attention because before my attention shifts to other things. Usually, your wife, children, and even your boss and colleagues can get your attention during the day and so by having a morning routine will ensure you deal with your most challenging tasks before they do.

When I started on business, I used to get distracted by meetings and other interruptions that I could not manage to do anything substantial. I decided to handle my personal projects very early in the morning and concentrate on them. Having that very few visitors could visit before 7 a.m., I managed to focus and realized that I now achieved more.

Handle Other Side Projects

Most of us have a side project that we wish we could work on, but do you find time for it? It is easy to skip your side hustles, after you have been through a busy day, feeling tired and exhausted. Most of the time the only thing on your mind is what you will have for dinner and sleep. For this reason, it is advisable to use some time in the morning before engaging in your day's work for your side project. In fact, most successful people do this.

I personally use my morning hours to prepare a religious book before going for my business. Through this, I can peruse and read through many articles and write some pages before going for my day's work. By creating time in the morning and write, and do it consistently, I can commit to its success.

Just like me, you should not forgo your personal projects; rather, you should use your mornings to do it before engaging in your daily activities.

Meditate

Our daily activities can make it difficult for us to have moments where we are free. It may be that your day is filled with engagements and always going up and down in the morning, that you are unable to do meditation.

However, regardless of how busy you are in the morning, find time to do meditation. Practice a habit of having a quiet moment when starting your day daily. You can spend that moment praying, meditating, reflect on your vision concerning the future, reflect on the positive things that you have gone through – or whatever you prefer. Having that short time quiet time offers you an excellent mindset to face your day.

Chapter 9:
Become More Productive in Less Time

Is there is an area of your life that needs self-discipline; it is in managing your time. Being able to manage your time is so instrumental in determining the kind of life you will live. It is hard to manage time, but by managing yourself, you will discover that your time is well spent.

Managing time involves managing your life rather than dealing with issues and circumstances. Time is perishable; it cannot be saved. Time is irreplaceable; nothing else can replace it. Time is irretrievable; once it is gone or wasted, you can never get it back. Finally, time is indispensable, especially for the accomplishment of any kind. All achievement, all results, all success requires time.

Now that it is evident that it is impossible to create time, the trick is to manage it in a different way. You can do this by spending your time in areas of your life where you prioritize more, instead of areas that have little or no value to you. This is the key to your achievement and the need to fully exercise self-discipline.

I Will Teach You to Master Self-Discipline

Time management involves having what it takes to choose the order of your events. By exercising self-discipline in how you spend your time, you will know what should happen first, followed by what and even what should be removed from your to-do list. This is a choice that you should make freely.

One of the habits that holds a lot of people back from being able to manage their life and ultimately time is procrastination. Procrastination has denied most people their great success and achievements. For you to overcome procrastination, you will need to exercise much self-discipline. Procrastination is a life snatcher. It steals all your dreams making you lose who you were meant to be.

There are some things in life that are more important than others. The challenge that a lot of people face is the most valuable things that we have committed ourselves to are hard and challenging. Most of the things that we find easy and enjoyable to do are more and have no meaningful impact on life. To know the importance of anything has in your life, look at the amount of time you have invested in it. It is common for people to pay attention and prioritize the one thing that they value most. For instance, I value exercise a lot, so part of my priorities when planning my day is ensuring I commit myself to at least 1 hour for workouts daily. To my friends who do not value exercise, that is crazy. By just looking at how someone spends time, you can know what he/she values.

The key to time management is having the discipline to put in place clear priorities and stick to them. Self-discipline is what will allow you to resist the habit of watching television when for instance you should be studying. How you spend your time is like your investment. Imagine you would be keen investing those 1 million dollars knowing that you will not get other money? You will apply all your knowledge to ensure that you get the best out of it. It's the same way you should do with your time to get the best return out of it.

We waste time through procrastination when we don't have self-discipline. You can find yourself wasting your valuable time on tasks that have little value and forego the one with high returns without realizing that what you do frequently becomes your habit. Most people have therefore developed a habit of procrastination, engaging in tasks that have no spoils and leaving the most important tasks unattended.

When developing discipline towards time management, you should ask yourself; what are the consequences if I don't finish this task or not? If you find that there will be serious effects when you don't complete it, them allocate it time to be completed and vice versa.

To better understand time management, have a look at the following tips:

Wake Up Early

Almost all successful people that I have met have one thing in common: they wake up early so that they can make better use of the day.

By this, they can have to prepare themselves to face the day. You can use the morning before you go to work to pray, meditate or do anything that may work for you before starting official duties. For those of you who like exercises like me, it will save a big deal.

Have A Schedule for Your Day's Goals?

By planning your daily work, you will be able to know what the day awaits you and make more efforts towards your goals. For you to be successful, you should realize the line between the high priority and urgent matters and those that can wait. This will help you to balance them during the day and leave those that are not urgent.

For my case, I work on the most important issues in the morning before looking at the emails and messages that have the potential to derail your progress. By breaking your tasks this way, you are to work towards your progress easily.

Some people advise that you split your time into two: focus time and buffer time. Focus time is when you should involve yourself in your main projects, whereas buffer time is for your small tasks. This can also help because you are able to give full concentration on your priority projects.

Avoid Multitasking

Are you serious? Yes, you heard me right. Multitasking might seem to be working towards your benefit, but in actual sense, it may be derailing you. The point here is when you do things at a slow pace you will put in all the necessary attention to all details and ultimately you will be more efficient and see more results. On the contrary, trying to accomplish a lot in a short period will make you overwhelmed leading to unnecessary stress.

Most of the people who prefer multitasking, miss having things done in the right manner. People tend to start so many things, but none of them are completed in the right manner. Instead of this, slow down a bit and focus fully on one goal at a time. By the time you are done, you will realize that no correction is required. This way you will move to your next project being proud that your former task is complete.

Create Deadlines for Your Goals

When you have set goals for yourself with definite deadlines, it will be easy to focus on their achievement. Lack of setting deadlines will make you think that you have a lot of time. Which is not always true because it can lead to procrastination.

Apart from the deadline that the client has given you, create your own short goals so that you will remain motivated to hit your target on time. If your deadline looks far away, you can break it into bits that you can achieve along the way. Focus on your small task at a time, and if you feel you are procrastinating, break it further to even smaller bits. Break them into smaller tasks to a point where it is hard to convince yourself that they are unattainable.

This is a trick used by many to avoid putting the whole project on hold until when the deadline is almost. You can also motivate yourself when you achieve your small projects. Find what motivates you and reward yourself.

Don't Be Hesitant in Acting

The mistake that all of us make at times is delaying taking actions when things arise. However, for you to save time and achieve more, have a habit of dealing with things as soon as they happen instead of waiting until when it is too late. Big problems always originate from small problems when left unattended for a long time. Therefore, don't make the mistake of ignoring a small matter when it arises before you may prevent the buildup of bigger issues that at the end will require more time to resolve.

Small issues that come in your way can be a hindrance to your progress when not solved. Always finish what you have started and when there arise some issues don't put them aside that you will deal with them later. For instance, maybe you are dealing with a project and realize there is something you have forgotten to include, don't tell yourself that you will come to it later. Resolve that issue and then move forward.

Avoid All Distractions

Are you the kind of person who usually gets distracted by phone or internet when working on your project? You can save yourself from that distraction by staying away from your phone and disable your computer notifications until when done with your work.

It is possible to get distracted by internal and external factors and sometimes you may be unintentionally using your distractors to escape from playing your role. It is paramount you understand what your distractors are and learn on ways you can avoid them. For instance, I usually turn off my phone and snooze all notifications during the time I am writing my project. This way I can stay focused for the time I have dedicated to my work. If you are working from an office, you can tell your secretary not to allow anyone in until when through. This will ensure your time is well spent by giving full attention to your goals.

Learn the Art of Saying NO

"NO" is a two-letter word but can determine whether you will be successful or not. Have you ever been in a situation where you feel that saying NO could have helped? I have many times. One day I was invited to a meeting that I felt I should not go. However, because now, I had not learned to say NO, I went for the sake of appeasing them. I was so frustrated in the meeting that when I look back today, I feel sorry for myself that I wasted my whole day instead of doing something productive. You may find yourself in a meeting and you are offered something that you don't like, but because of your inability to say no, you spend a lot of time trying to refuse the offer without offending anyone.

Again, as much as saying "No" is important, the same way saying "YES" is paramount for your success.

Delegate Some Duties

One is better than one. Sometimes you will be forced to delegate some of your projects as a way of time management. However, this should be done more carefully because it is paramount to delegate your work to the most qualified persons. When you have a great team, it will be easier for you to accomplish more within a short duration of time.

Chapter 10:
Why You Procrastinate in Explained in 15 Minutes

Are you not frustrated when there is something to be done, but you can't do or have the motivation to do it? Most people procrastinate at a point in their life, however for some people it has become a habit to procrastinate on anything that needs to be done. But have you ever asked yourself what makes you procrastinate and not do the things that are more important but instead do things that have the least importance? It is really tempting to watch your favorite movie instead of doing that assignment.

The major reason that makes it challenging to deal with procrastination is, because each person has a different reason for procrastinating. Each person has several reasons for procrastinating on different things. Excuses that procrastinators give are so similar. First, they always think that they will have time to do a task. Although this is not always true because there is a habit of postponing and when the time they had postponed to comes, they will still give the same excuse. Sometimes they will claim they are held up, and so they cannot commit to doing a task. They know they need to exercise, but they will claim they can't get time for it now.

For you to stop procrastinating and get things done immediately, you must know the reasons why you are procrastinating. Through this, you will be able to handle it and even eliminate this habit.

Without going further, check the following reasons as to why you procrastinate:

You Are Afraid of The Unknown
Most of us fear stepping out to get things done because we are not sure what the results would be. For instance, you may be having a health concern that you are afraid that when you go to the hospital and get the problem diagnosed, the results may be traumatizing. So, you prefer to stay with your condition hoping that it will just go away on its own. Sometimes you are afraid that by taking that step, some truths that you are not willing to bear will come to light.

I disagree with the saying that says that "what you don't know won't hurt you". This is because when you assume a problem it will get worse and you will be too late when you realize that.

When you allow misconception to control your mind, it will influence the way you think, and you won't be able to act even when you know you are headed the wrong direction. You will go on living in misconception, particularly if it lines with what you believe. You will in misconception tell yourself that this thing will pass away on its own with time or none of my family members has gone through this before, and so I am fine.

But think about this what if for instance you are talking about a disease like cancer that can be handled in its early stages? Would it be better to act early than wait?

Fear to Make A Mistake

Most people procrastinate because they think that in stepping out and do something, if they fail, they will expose themselves. They believe in perfection. Do you find yourself failing to do things because you fear making mistakes? It is so dangerous as it can lead to procrastination.

Anything that you find yourself doing is a product of your mindset. For you to succeed in any area of your life, be it in athletics, arts or even music, your minds must be set for success. You can either have a "fixed mindset" or a "growth mindset". When you possess a "fixed mindset", you tend to believe that your abilities are limited and it's probable that you will not experience growth. On the other hand, those with a ``growth mindset" believe that they are limitless and can develop and prosper by working hard. They believe that they have unlimited abilities and can step out without concentrating on failure.

When you fear making mistakes, you will only do things that you believe are in line with your perfection and avoid tasks that would require you to put a little more effort to accomplish. Although some may argue that this is a good trait, it is so harmful to you and a great enemy of progress.

Fear of Success

Yes!! Some of the reasons that you procrastinate are because you fear the pressure that comes with succeeding. Sometimes you may feel that when you succeed people will expect more from you going forward. Or that when you succeed, you will be known by many people and maybe you prefer a private life.

Most often, this kind of procrastination happens to people who have low self-esteem, and so their worth is mostly tied to their achievements. You may find yourself challenging yourself on how much you should put up so that you can be perfect. And so, any achievement will mean more expectations to your minds.

Over time this may lead to you losing identity and sometimes you don't feel like you own your success. This will ultimately lead to procrastination as a way of avoiding the pressure of always trying to be better.

Thinking That You Can Do It Later

Do you get telling yourself that you will do a certain task later? If you said yes, watch out because you may be a victim of procrastination. This is a lie that shows that in the time to come you will have a perfect opportunity to carry out your task.

It may be that you wanted to do exercises in the morning before going to work. But your minds tell you that the best time to do it is in the evening after finishing your duties. This may sound like good advice in the morning, but the reality is when evening comes, you may be tired and hitting the gym may be difficult.

What you may not know is that your mind is trying to give solace now at the expense of your goals and dreams. Again, your mind changes with time and whatever you have decided you will do later, or date may be subject to the state of mind that you will be when that time comes.

Working on Easier Tasks
This is common to most people. It is easier for you to browse through Facebook and emails rather than settle on that research project. How many times have you found yourself talking with your colleague instead of working?

Think of the many easier tasks that you have put in place when you don't feel like dealing with real issues. Although these tasks tend to make you busy and engaged, it is just a form of procrastination you've created. The reason why you find yourself engaging in easier tasks is that you can finish them quickly and have an instant sense of fulfillment. The more challenging and harder a task is, the more time you will need to do, and chances are you may engage in procrastination and avoid them. This is because you may see the benefit as being so far.

Lack of Motivation
Most of the time I have people say that I don't like what I am doing. If you have a habit of doing only things that you feel motivated to do, there are high chances that you procrastinate a lot. This is because

most of the things that you may find on your to-do list may not motivate you. For instance, waking at 5.00 a.m. and have a walk before going to your work is not an easy thing and you will need self-discipline to achieve that.

Your attitude towards a task could be working against you achieving your goals. What do you think when the idea of stepping out and do something strikes you? If you feel that laziness strikes when you are supposed to do something, then your attitude is coming in the way of your success. You should have ways to tackle that if you are to succeed. Imagine if you depend on what you feel so that you could do anything? Most things would remain undone because our minds would easily avoid challenging tasks.

Lack of Knowledge to Complete A Task

When you don't have the necessary skills to start and complete a task, you are most likely to procrastinate on it. For instance, if you are given a task to write a book and you don't have the skills required to handle it, it is probable that you might avoid that task.

Due to human nature, you may not even have the courage to inquire, and so the only option for you will be to procrastinate. Your mind will be inclined to avoid the task instead of going out and learning the skills to do that task. At some point, I was a victim of this in my life especially when with my friends. I preferred not to do something that I was unsure of instead of doing it the wrong way and appear dumb to them. Here you will use procrastination as a defense against being mocked when you lack the required skills to do a certain task.

Lack of Interest

When you lack interest in doing a certain task, there are high chances that you will start procrastinating. All of us, on some occasions, lack interest in things that we are supposed to do, but this should not automatically imply that you stop doing that thing.

When you don't have an interest in your goals, it is easy to get distracted with other things that have little benefits that may appear more appealing to you now. For example, you may have an assignment that you are supposed to do, but because you don't have an interest, you may start playing games or browsing the internet. This will lead to procrastination, and before you discover it, you will have wasted a lot of time. You can avoid this kind of procrastination by forcing yourself in activities that you are not interested if they are supposed to be done.

You Are Easily Distracted

Are easily distracted by text messages, social media, Skype, phone, emails, etc.? Distraction is affecting the productivity of employees more than can you imagine. These distractions eat into your time making you procrastinate on doing your most important duties. That time when you are browsing the internet or make an unrelated phone call, you could use it to make your goals a reality.

It is easy for you to give in to distractions depending on the kind of task you are dealing with. When you are doing a challenging or difficult task, and for instance, a message from your friend appears on the screen, you will be tempted to look at the message to avoid that challenging task. Therefore, keeping yourself away from all distractions will help, especially if you are not disciplined enough to say no to distractions.

You Always Avoid Hard and Challenging Tasks

Sometimes we tend to avoid tasks that need a lot of effort. Some projects will also require you to give up on some habits for you to accomplish them. For instance, if you are working towards losing weight, you will be required to work extra hard and even wake up early so that you could have time for exercises. There are also some foods that you will require to stop taking like junk foods and fatty foods.

If you are not very serious about losing weight, you may use this as an excuse to procrastinate and avoid putting up with exercises. A project can be challenging in that it requires your patience for you to achieve it. Losing weight is not something that you can achieve overnight. Also, most successful business persons employed patience to reach where they are today. It is easy for you to procrastinate after realizing that it will take quite some time before you realize your goals. People like instant rewards and results. By procrastinating, you will find other simple activities to engage in instead of putting the necessary effort to achieve your goals.

Chapter 11:
Over Come Procrastination Through Self-Discipline

In the immediate chapter, we have looked at what causes us to procrastinate on our goals. In this chapter, we are going to look at methods you can use to stop procrastinating. We all find ourselves in this situation: the deadline to a task is approaching, but instead of using any time we have towards achieving our goal, we find ourselves engaging in less meaningful activities like social media, playing games, browsing through the internet and checking emails. You understand you should be doing a task, but you are not in the mood to do it.

Procrastination is common to people of all classes. When procrastinating, you tend to avoid the important things you should be doing until when the deadline is too close, you are overwhelmed and wish you could have started earlier.

Some people are so much in procrastination that they tend to postpone everything in their life and always remain in the same cycle. When you have a habit of putting things off, avoiding work and only working when the task in question is not avoidable, you will never achieve anything great in life. The good thing is there is a solution if you carefully exercise the following:

Break Your Goals into Small Bits

As said in an earlier chapter, one of the major reasons that people procrastinate is because they have a huge work log that they feel overwhelmed. By breaking your project into smaller portions, you will be able to concentrate on one portion at a time. If when working on those portions that you have broken, you still procrastinate, break your project into even smaller portions. When you do this, you will not have any excuse to delay doing your project.

For instance, if you are planning to start a supply business that will cover the whole country, you can plan your business in such a way that you will start your supply in the capital city first. Later, after covering the capital city, you can go on to another town. Through this, it will be easier to concentrate on each portion of the project without being highly overwhelmed.

Have a plan on how you will progress in your project until you cover the whole country by having manageable parts of the project. Concentrate on each phase without thinking on other parts until when you are through with it, and then you can move to the next.

Have A Strong Reason Why You Must Act?

One of the main reasons that we procrastinate is because we focus on our short-term fulfillment or benefits. We tend to avoid the stress that comes with staying committed and instead enjoy the short-term pleasure that comes with it, not knowing that it may bring long term suffering by not acting. You should focus on the benefits you will get on doing that task no matter how hard or uncomfortable you may be when doing it.

If, for instance, you are aiming to lose weight. Imagine how comfortable and healthy you will feel when you have attained the weight you so much desire. If it is a business, visualize the profits you will get when you have got things going. Instead of focusing on the sacrifice that you will make to achieve your goals, visualize the product.

This will not only make you motivated but will help you to focus on the final prize or reward. When you keep your mind on the reward it will be easy for you to stop procrastinating and get things going.

Be Realistic When Setting Your Goals

When setting your goals, you must be realistic. Set in place doable and achievable goals. It is good to aim higher, but don't make the mistake of aiming what is not achievable. Be realistic in the amount of time you give yourself to complete your tasks. Setting very short deadlines than what can be possibly achieved will only lead to frustration.

Projects tend to take more time than we anticipated and so give yourself enough time to complete the project. I don't know what you think will happen when you don't have enough time to complete a task. It feels awful and overwhelming. When overwhelmed your mind may tend to tell you that the only option is to avoid doing the task because you will not succeed within the deadline you have set yourself.

If you are starting on exercises, you must start with light exercises like walking for 10-20 minutes in the morning. When you set yourself for huge tasks at the start, you may find yourself giving up before you even start. Therefore, being realistic in terms of the task and the time within which you want to accomplish a task will enable you to achieve your goals and avoid procrastinating.

Remove Distractions

When working towards stopping procrastinating, you must keep your environment from all distractions. Your environment can hinder your growth. Remove all distractions, especially the ones that you know can tempt you easily. In my case, I usually keep away from social media when working on a project because they can distract me easily.

The kind of environment that you are working on is determinant of the work you will do. Look at how your office or room is arranged. How is your desk arranged? Anything that you feel can make your attention to shift, change it. During the time that you have set to work on a task, remove all distractions. Sometimes you will be forced to switch off your phone, snooze notifications on your desktop and avoid talking to your colleagues when you should be working. Let your mind be focused on finishing your project first before engaging in any other task. Through this, you will give all your attention to the task, and you will achieve more.

Exercise Self-Forgiveness

Are you the kind of person who usually beats yourself up does to past mistakes? You better stop because that may be the reason you are always procrastinating. Saying negative things towards yourself will only lead to frustration. Saying things like "I always waste time" or " I am always a loser" is so detrimental towards your progress. Even when you have procrastinated in the past, forgive yourself so that you can be able to deal on your current task well.

Make use of your experience with procrastination to your advantage. You can do this by trying to ask yourself what caused you to procrastinate on your past project or task. Is it stress, distractions or lack of skills? What it is that you find makes you procrastinate? Find ways to address them at that moment going forward. If it is lack of skills that made you avoid tasks, you should put in place measures to learn more skills so that in the future you will not procrastinate.

Also, by forgiving yourself, you will give yourself an opportunity to refocus and handle things differently. If you find that your avoidance is due to putting wrong priorities or unrealistic goals, you will be able to come up with good plans. You will also have peace of mind and confidence that is so instrumental in your moving forward.

Stop Giving Excuses

Most of the time we are held back by excuses. Do you find yourself saying the following things? 'I will visit you once I have time", " I am not in the mood", "I wish so and so could be here, I could do this" and the like? You need to refrain from that habit if you opt to move forward and achieve your goals.

You must be realistic to yourself and realize whether they are good reasons holding you back, or it is just an excuse. We tend to use excuses when we want to avoid acting and not feel guilty. So, we hold on excuses and convince ourselves that we have a good reason for not doing what we were supposed to do. We all find it good to be in the mood when doing something, but we should not allow that to stand in our way of achievements.

Some of the things that present a lot of benefits are not motivating and so waiting until when you are in the mood may mean that you will never do them. Waking up early so that you can find time to do your side project is not an easy thing. But when you decide and do it the benefits will be so pleasing. This means you must act even when your emotions are saying otherwise.

Don't Keep Your Goals Secret

Although some people prefer keeping their goals secret. When you want to stop procrastinating, this may not apply. When you know that no one knows about your plans, it may be easy to sleep over them and not act because there is no one will put you into account when you don't achieve them. I recommend that you share your goals and dreams with someone who will hold you into account when you don't complete what you had purposed.

This can be your partner, your teacher or even your boss. Sometimes you will also need to look for a coach who will ensure that you are doing what is expected. A perfect instance is when you are working towards losing weight. You will need to have a coach who will guide you on the kind of exercises you should do. You may also need to have a nutritionist who will guide you towards achieving your goal. With all these people to monitor you, you will be forced to put all the necessary efforts so that you succeed because you know you will be ashamed in the case you fail.

Avoid Perfectionism

Do you tend to believe you are nothing when you fail, or you are something when you succeed? This is not a good mentality. This is a mentality that shows that you are either perfect or nothing. People with this mentality wait until when the situation is perfect for them to do something. They are always in search of the perfect time to begin an assignment or start a business. Waiting until you are 100% sure that what you are about to do will succeed may translate that you will not start at all. This mentality can hold you back and taking steps towards starting a project may be impossible.

Instead of this mentality, you should focus on doing your best. This means that you will work your best towards a goal.

To avoid procrastinating when planning to start a project, don't focus on finding the perfect time, perfect place or anything perfect – you may never find it, rather concentrate on better. For instance, you may never find a perfect place to start a business, but you can find a better place. Through this, you will not waste your time on where to get a perfect place, but rather use that energy towards promoting development.

Look for Role Models

Anything that you are trying to accomplish it is probable that there are people who have gone through it and succeeded. Let's say you are trying to lose fat and you are at the verge of procrastinating, finding someone who has been through it will motivate you to work harder. Connect with them and learn what secrets they used in hitting their target.

Knowing that upon putting in the necessary effort towards your goals you can achieve them will motivate you a lot. One of the reasons that people procrastinate is because they think that their situation is unique and that no one has been there before. But by moving out and seeking mentors, you will be astonished when you learn that others have been there and succeeded.

Don't Take Long to Plan – Act

I Will Teach You to Master Self-Discipline

One of the reasons that most people procrastinate is because they take a lot of time in the planning process. Think about how much time you have been planning to work on your diet, to stop complaining or even start that new business. Over planning can easily lead to inaction. You may strategize, plan and hypothesize, but if no action is put in place, nothing will be achieved.

It is easy for you to sit down and complain, but the question that you should ask yourself is; what are you doing to change your situation? Take actions now, and before you know it, success will be knocking your way- Stop Procrastinating!

Chapter 12:
Growth Mindset to Achieve Anything

Our mindset affects how we act and our potential for acting. People who have a mindset that can be improved through hard work, learning, improving strategies and even change of environment, have a growth mindset. They achieve more than those individuals that have a fixed mindset. People with a growth mindset are not bothered when they start small because they believe they can navigate through hard work and improved strategies and experience success.

People possess a mix of both a fixed and growth mindset — the mindset changes depending on the environment, circumstances and the type of hardships we are facing. Our mindsets can also be affected by the way we were brought up because children minds are easy to change during upbringing.

Mindset is so important because it determines what we will achieve in life. Therefore, you need to guard your mindset by having a clear view of your growth. Ask yourself, what pushes you towards growth? Is it when facing challenges? When taking risks? Or even when comfortable. By doing this, you will know how to avoid having a fixed mindset.

Many things affect our mindset, and so we need to be so careful about things that we embrace. People that have a growth mindset and exercise it more regularly can find ways to avoid old bad habits. This is because their minds are always finding solutions. With a growth mindset, you can embrace change and are open to different ideas.

Long-term thinking is so instrumental in developing self-discipline and succeeding in life. When you look at the business giants in the world, they all had a long-term plan for their business that enabled them to reach their current levels. Therefore, if you are dreaming of succeeding in life and being different from your peers, you must embrace long-term thinking. When you think long-term and have a plan to reach there, although what you do daily may not seem to show results, but slowly, you will make strides towards your goals.

Imagine when you were a child when your parents gave you a small amount of money to use on whatever that may interest you. Your only thought was to go directly to the shop and buy your favorite toy or popcorn. This is because you were more concerned with immediate satisfaction. There was no reason not to do that because you depended on your parents to give more money any time you needed.

As you grow older, it is probable that your parents would give allowances frequently, instead of giving you instant cash upon request.

Edgar D. Moranis

Your parents could give a monthly amount that he expected to take you for a specific period, let's say a month. This means that, when you wanted to do something, you first had to think, because when the money that you had been given runs out before the time to be given additional money came, you would suffer. This shows that for you to survive, you had to think long-term rather than always giving in to your short-term satisfaction.

Most people, especially those who work on monthly basis fall into the temptation of not thinking long-term. Having that they expect their salary every month, they tend to spend all their money on recurrent expenditure because they know that after 30 days or anytime, they receive their pay they will get other money. They spend all their income on their monthly needs such as paying the electricity bill, rent, buying food and even entertainment. This cycle can repeat itself month after month because it offers short-term satisfaction and is comfortable.

But that kind of strategy cannot allow you progress in life and that is why you must have in place long-term thinking.

Long-term thinking is very significant in assessing where your life is headed and in building self-discipline. No wonder you will find most employers asking the interviewees their long-term goals before hiring. This is because they know employees with long-term goals are more focused and disciplined and so working with them will lead to the success of their companies too. A long-term thinking person is goal-oriented.

One of the reasons that you find yourself obsessing on setbacks rather than focus on the long-term goals is because your minds are focused on obstacles instead of the future that you aim for.

How Long-Term Thinking Helps You Build Self-Discipline and Enhances Your Progress

When you start thinking long-term, it will be easy to build self-discipline and progress in life as opposed to thinking short-term as you will see below.

You will Move Forward Instead of Being Caught in Problems for Long

One of the reasons that we are held back is because we tend to be caught up by challenges. You should not allow what is currently taking place in your life to make you forget your long-term goals. We all pass through challenges when working on something. Many times, it is possible to think that the challenges that we are facing are an indication that we should not go ahead with our plans. However, you ought to remain focused and determined even when things get tough.

When things get tough, remind yourself that opportunities come dressed in ways that are not always pleasing. Imagine how treasure is buried in the ground and it is only the hardworking and determined that will get hold of them. Having long-term thinking will enable you to go beyond your setbacks to achieve your goals. It enables you to remain disciplined and anchored onto your goals even when things get tough.

You Don't Measure Life by Looking at Your Failures

One of the things that bring down people with short-term thinking is that they use their setbacks and failures to measure their life. But when you are thinking long-term, you will be able to avoid paying much attention to your failures because you will visualize yourself getting over them.

People with short-term thinking tend to be distracted by their setbacks so much that they forget their goals. They overstay on their failures thinking that it is over. They have a keen eye on the negative things happening in their life that they can't do anything. But, when you have long-term thinking, although you have setbacks, you will remember your long-term goals which will help you to remain focused. It is true that you will be faced by real setbacks, but through your long-term mentality, you will gather all your efforts towards your success.

You Will Remain Focused on the Final Prize

I Will Teach You to Master Self-Discipline

It takes self-discipline to wake up every morning and go to the gym even when you don't see quick results. With long-term thinking, you don't focus on how slow you are moving provided you are making progress. Long-term thinking also allows you to avoid taking things too seriously because you know that through patient a solution would be found.

People with short-term thinking lack a clear picture of the future they hope for. They easily give in when they are faced with hardships. Instead of concentrating on your failures, always visualize your future. We all go through tough moments in life, and although this may subject us to a lot of discomfort, they allow for essential growth for the goal before us.

You Will Be Constrained in Your Abilities

One of the differences between those people that think short-term and those that think long-term is that those that think short term is always constrained to their abilities currently whereas those that think long-term are not. For instance, when thinking short-term, you will not think beyond your financial ability, language, muscle ability and many other things. This means that when drafting their vision, it will be limited to their knowledge and abilities now. For instance, you may be dreaming of building a palatial house. When thinking short-term, your minds will argue that it is not possible to build that house because you will not be able to visualize yourself having money in the future. Through this, their dream will become weak, and eventually, their dreams will diminish.

However, when thinking long-term, you will be able to get over all limitations and step out into action. Long-term thinking allows you to believe that you will achieve any dream in your life no matter your limitations now. It allows you to navigate through and look for ways that will make you achieve by removing anything standing in the way.

People who think long-term is not easily affected by their surroundings, unlike short-term thinkers who will be affected by every detail of their surroundings. Long-term thinkers decide and stick no matter what they go through. For instance, if you have decided to start a blog, you will not allow anything to stand in your way. Even if you don't have much knowledge on the subject that you want to write, you will find the knowledge instead of doing the easier thing which is to quit or change your minds. You will make all the effort so that you could achieve.

Unfortunately, this is not what happens with short-term thinkers. They are affected by their surrounding including what their friends tell them. And if they happen to talk negative about their plans, they are likely to quit. For you to succeed in anything you have dreamed off, and not be affected by your surroundings, think long-term.

Long-term Thinking enables You to Be Patient

I Will Teach You to Master Self-Discipline

One fundamental principle for success is patience. All successful people have taken a lot of time to reach their destination. No huge thing can be built in a day. Imagine the time it took for brands like Amazon to grow to their present levels! It took a lot of time and patience was paramount. Without patience, it is possible to quit halfway, or at any point, you feel discouraged.

It is common for business or anything that you have started not to show results during the first stages. If you don't have long-term thinking, you can easily quit at this point. This is because your short-term thinking might show you that the project is not realistic or is unachievable. However, that is a test for your patience.

Therefore, you must learn to wait for the foundation of your project to become strong. Long-term thinking is so instrumental in ensuring that you can endure the current pain and disappointments for the sake of your long-term goals. But, when thinking short-term, you may grow impatient and even quit. Short-term thinking is after overnight success. Having that this is not always possible, it may become detrimental to your success.

When you have well laid up plans and constantly working towards your goals, patience will be a significant component of your success. You can only achieve this by thinking long-term so that you can understand why every significant growth need time.

Edgar D. Moranis

You will develop essential characters like self-discipline and self-control when you continuously think long-term. With time you will find that you no longer struggle to do the right thing. Your mind will be set in a way that your goal and dreams are very important than your instant pleasures and satisfaction and therefore you will easily step out and act. You will see how every step you are taking is drawing you closer to your goals.

Chapter 13:
The Future is Brighter Than You Think

A motivational speaker Jim Rohm once said that " You are the average of the five people you spend the most time with". Although one can claim to have personal choices, the people that we spend time with plays a significant role in our behaviors, attitudes and beliefs. You can't argue the fact that people have a great impact on your behavior. That is why you hear things like peer pressure. Social groups are the determiner of norms and culture. It is therefore important to be keen on the impact of your associations on your behavior and success.

The Power of Associations

Anytime I think about the impact of our friends on our life, I remember a Chinese proverb that goes ``three men make a tiger''. In that story, the king is asked whether he would believe when one or two citizens claim that a tiger was roaming in the city streets. The king said no. But when asked whether he would believe when three or more people repeated the same thing, interesting he said he would believe. Those around him were astonished and reminded them that it was impossible for a tiger to roam in the streets no matter how many people said so.

What do you take from that? It means that if there is many people arguing about something is true, no make how unrealistic it is, their argument might be accepted at the end. Therefore, you might find yourself agreeing to what most of your friends are saying. No matter how much you may try to remain the one with a different opinion, most of the time you might find yourself giving in. There is an attitude that is within your association, and no matter how you try to google or inquire from other sources it might not be easy to go against your associations.

The only way you can help yourself from negative impact that may arise from your association is to wisely choose who you spend most of your time with. Ask yourself, are my associations leading an interesting life, or are a negative life? Some people possess a limiting attitude and behaviors. They are dull, have negative imaginations and not interesting to stay with. You can shape your life by staying away from such people. Imagine you are planning to do exercises and change how your appearance, but your association is so negative regarding exercises. No matter how you try, it will be hard to continue exercising. They will always limit you and show how exercises will not work. This might cause you think that you are wasting your time. On the contrary, if you always hook up with people who are doing exercises, you will always feel motivated, and you will not struggle much to wake up and exercise.

Having the right association allows you to remain focused and passionate instead of going through one idea to another through life. This is because your association will be instrumental in ensuring that you are encouraged to move on no matter how tough it becomes. You will always have a strong opinion about life, and you will have a huge impact on the world. When waking up in the morning, you will be full of energy and full of enthusiasm.

Remember you are more likely to believe what three or more people say. Therefore, if many your associations have a negative attitude, you are going to be affected. If they say something is not possible which is mostly due to their limiting attitude, you are likely to join them in tune. If you spend time with people who always hang on social media, even if you aren't a fan of social media, you might be forced to change for you to fit in that group. If you spend time with people who believe their dreams are unachievable, you might as well believe that yours too are mere imaginations. Associating your life with people who focuses more on limitations and negativity, will do you more harm.

Imagine if you would surround yourself with people with the following mindsets:

People Who Always Says "I Can't Do"

The most detrimental imagination you can have towards yourself is to think that you can't achieve something. Having this kind of thought alone is so harmful that it can make you stop pursuing your goals and work on something else. It is obvious that you put your efforts on what you think you can accomplish. You should keep yourself away from people with this kind of mindset. When you are having a chat with your friends and hear them say that the reason, they are not working towards their goals is because they can't make it, know that you are associating yourself with a very dangerous character. These people will always give excuses as to why they can't make it. Associating yourself with these people might make you lose inspiration to work on your dreams.

People Who Think They Are Not Good Enough

There are some people who think that they are inferior in handling their tasks. They think that they don't have what it takes to act. Usually, this is not regarding their talents but is as a result of much negative comparison to other people. This can be so demoralizing not just to them but also to the people around them.

If you want to realize your goals, there are not the right people to hang with. Spending a lot of time with such people can make you have inferior thoughts about yourself. Surround yourself with people who have faith in themselves and believes that they can stand up and do something. Through this, you will be inspired to fight for your dreams.

Sometimes the going may get tough, but when you have the right company, you will find things a bit easier.

People Who Anticipate Bad Things "What Ifs."

It is true that when indulging in something new, you will want to know the outcome. But, associating yourself with people who always think negative concerning the future is wrong. This is because those people who always are always thinking that negative things will happen, don't act. Imagine having people around you who always see something happening. You tell them you a new business idea, and the only thing that comes from their mouth is "what if it doesn't work?". It will be so challenging for you to go on with your plan.

Surrounding yourself with people who always possibility and positivity will help you to start something and succeed. It is probable that some of your goals that you have not embarked on are because you associated yourself with uninspiring people. Although many may argue that life is not certain, it could not be logic to always think negatively. Life involves taking risks. Therefore, ensure your associations are people who can inspire you to be better by taking risks. This cannot happen if you or your associates are always thinking negative.

They Are Perfectionists

Imagine staying with people who fear making mistakes, and it can be so limiting. Trying to make every detail of your life perfect can be so draining. Again, it limits someone from making any progress in life.

Staying with this kind of people might mean that you will never step out and try anything. And obviously, without trying anything, it will be impossible for you to achieve. Talk to any great achievers, and you will be astonished on how many times they tried and failed before they could succeed. No man does not make mistakes, and so no one should stop trying for fear of making mistakes. People who put much attention on being perfect, usually miss out on taking risks. They limit themselves and usually get trapped in a comfort zone.

What separates ordinary people from those whose progress is their ability to accept failure and move one. This means if you want to achieve more in life, you should check on your associations. If they happen to fear failure that it limits them from taking steps, avoid them as much as possible.

The Effects of Having Positive People Around You

The impacts you will get when you surround yourself with positive and interesting people will be astounding. People with interesting things happening in their life are so energetic and enthusiastic. When your associations are positive individuals, your attitude will be great and have a good approach towards life.

People who are working towards their dreams are risk takers and are confident that they will be successful. They have high hopes concerning their future and are willing to take any step so that they can succeed. This is the type of people you should be exposed to regularly so that you could be successful. One of the benefits that you will gain when you associate yourself with these people is that you will have a great attitude and behavior.

When these people to go forward, you will be more inspired to do the same. You will start to realize the kind of things you can do in your life. For instance, when you look at people who have been successful in the profession or business that you are planning to start, it will help you know that your dream is achievable. Understanding how they tackled the kind of hardships they faced in their journey will help you remain inspired. One of the reasons that people give up is because they think the challenges, they are facing are unique and that no one has gone through and succeeded. But, when you have people to look up to, it will be hard for you to not give up.

Different people have different ideas concerning the world. People have different passions and talents and so interacting with inspiring people will expose you to new experiences and ideas. The secret is to surround yourself with the right people.

How Do You Take Control of People in Your Life?

Know Your Goals

It is your responsibility to choose the kind of people you would like around you. You can easily do this by identifying your dreams and then hooking up with people that you believe will be instrumental in moving them forward. This can be a mentor or people that you believe offers the necessary support in terms of both attitude, behavior and skills. Having some clear deliberations for your goals will help you to have the right associations and will be important for your success.

Find Same-Minded Groups

People working towards the same purpose or target usually encounter the same problems. Therefore, engaging yourself with the same-minded people will help you remain focused and enhance personal development. In this group, people encourage each other, challenge each other and even find solutions.

If you can't find one such group around you, you can create one.

Act Like Individuals You Want to Interact With

You are likely to attract individuals that you share the same traits. If you like blogging, it is probable that you will attract other bloggers. If you are a bodybuilder, you will attract people who love workouts. This implies that after you have identified people that you want to interact with, learn their behaviors and act like them, though not blindly. For instance, in my daily travels, I have found myself easily interacting with people due to my love for sports. It has been my main conversation starter, and it also determines the kind of people I interact with.

Avoid Excuses

The time I have involved myself with positive people, I have realized they have controlled thoughts. They merely make excuses and does their best to execute their plans and achieve their goals. If you want to attract such people, you must be accountable and have control of your minds. It will be insane to think that you can live carelessly and then expect to attract inspiring people near you.

Avoid the Negative

You need to avoid the harmful thoughts and voices that distracts you from moving forward. Minimize the time you spend with people who usually criticize you. Avoid the people who lead to places you don't wish to be. Your thoughts are so important and should be guarded in any way possible.

Not just the people that you interact with physically can have an impact on your life. The magazines and books you constantly read can affect the way you read. Things that you read on the internet can also determine how your minds will think. Avoid reading content that will weigh you down. Don't allow your minds to be exposed to a lot of garbage as this will affect you badly.

Having the right people around will help you know when you are going the wrong direction, motivate you when you feel weighed down and greatly inspire you when trying to hit your target.

Eliminating Distractions from Your Environment So You Can Focus on What's Important

It is possible for you to be distracted in your work due to the many distractions available. From people to phones to the internet, so many other things can easily distract you when you ought to remain focused and productive. Distractions are so detrimental in that they make you miss deadlines and have little time to rest. Eventually, this will make you exhausted and unable to give proper attention to your work and fail to deliver your full potential.

It is easy for you to be distracted by the internet or any other distraction without knowing. Sometimes you may tell yourself - with this digital era you cannot stay away from your phone or the internet. However, before you know it, you have wasted a lot of time that you could use to do your work. If you can manage to eliminate distractions in your work, it will be easy to be focused on your goals and eventually you will achieve more.

However, for you to eliminate distractions, you should embrace the following tips:

Tips You Can Use to Eliminate Distractions

Make Your Schedule
It is easy for you to give in to distractions if you miss a proper work schedule. Having a work schedule allows you to say "NO" to too many things if not on your plan. Without a schedule, you are bound to make a lot of steps that are uncalled for and eventually find it hard to

accomplish your dreams. So, the key to eliminating distractions is to have a schedule for your day and avoid deviating from it.

Have Enough Rest

One of the perfect ways to make sure that you get enough rest is to get enough sleep. Sometimes it is not easy, but it is crucial for the body. Having enough sleep gives you a better day as compared to taking coffee in the morning. A better point to start having enough sleep is to have a proper sleep schedule. Ensure you sleep enough hours, usually 7-9 hours. You can make it possible by avoiding activities that keep you awake past your scheduled sleep time. This includes avoiding things like watching tv or even overworking.

Take Healthy Diet

Always find time to eat healthily. Satisfying our cravings with donuts and junk foods is easy. However, just like our body, the brains need energy so that they can work well. Anytime you feel hungry, eat food that will give your brains energy and help you remain focused throughout the day. Through this, it will be easy to avoid being distracted.

Ensure Your Working Space is Clean

Imagine what seeing that disorganized working desk does to your mind. It causes a lot of distraction. Ensure your working space is organized so that you can minimize distractions. Whatever working space you are on, ensure it is orderly so that your work can be easily done.

Off course you can decorate your workspace with what you like but ensure it does not go overboard.

Snooze Social Notifications on Your Computer

We all know the important role that computers play in our work. However, when not carefully monitored it can be a very big source of distraction. Imagine working on your computer while social notifications are peeping on your screen? It will be very hard for you to ignore them and continue with work. Therefore, for you to remain focused on your important work, it will be better to snooze the notifications. This will enable you to put all the necessary attention to your work and achieve more.

To ensure you don't miss anything important, you can't take small breaks and check on slack, emails or any other media.

Switch the Phone Off

Looking at your phone's messages, playing games and making calls can be a big source of distraction. Therefore, switching it off and keeping away can be a great way to avoid distractions on your work.

Make People Aware You're Busy Working

Although it may seem obvious, letting people know you are working is important in eliminating distractions. The time you dedicated to work should be known to all your friends and relatives. Tell your co-workers that you don't want disturbances in a certain period for you to concentrate well. If you have a secretary, it will be easier for you because you can give her instructions not to allow visitors for the said period. You also put a sign if you feel that will keep people away. This will ensure you achieve more daily.

Exercising the above tips will be instrumental in ensuring you are not distracted. Now you can sit down and work. Also, ensure you have all the tools you may need so that you will not take much time looking for them. Avoiding distractions will ensure that you achieve more.

Chapter 14:
My Number One Method to Build Self-Discipline (It Actually Works)

Self-discipline involves doing things that we don't like so that we can achieve our goals. It requires self-discipline to take the right food and do workouts. It is not easy to avoid eating chips or that donut you love so much. It needs regular practice and dedication for you to achieve it. Just like you improve each day on exercises as you practice, so you get used to eating the right food even if you don't like it.

When I wanted to lose weight, I knew I had to do something with my diet. I always felt uncomfortable, and I felt embarrassed most of the time. Concentration was becoming a problem and before I knew it my life was a mess. I realized I had to eat healthy not only for the sake of losing weight but also to have enough for my mind. Obviously, the challenge was not to stop eating more but to eat the right food, which I didn't like at all — but looking at the benefits that were at stake I had to try bit by bit to change.

The journey wasn't easy but a real struggle. I had to struggle each day. This is because one part of myself felt that I needed to change for my good while the other showed me that I was sacrificing my liking for the sake of the future. It is true that I needed to be healthy once again, but it was hard to overcome the strong urge of what I loved. It is much easier to replace what you don't like with what you do, but doing the opposite requires dedication and self-discipline.

This meant that I had to change how I perceived food. I knew that I needed my small weight back and so I had to do anything to achieve it. I had to work on my perception. I decided to value my body and decided if losing weight means eating what I didn't like, let it be so. I started taking the food I didn't like no matter the urge I had for sugary foods and chips. At first, it was not easy, but I constantly reminded myself of the benefits ahead. This made me step out further against my will. Having realized that our minds are not always set for success, but it is a practice that if embraced can bring results, I worked towards it.

After practicing the habit of eating what I don't like for a long time, I found that I no longer had many struggles in doing it. It now became much easier to eat the right food and my urge for sugary and junk foods reduced. This meant that I was now more in control of my life than before. I realized if I had done the easier thing of eating only what I liked no matter how harmful it was for my body; I could still be struggling with overweight.

After winning my bad eating habits, I realized that I was more disciplined in many areas of my life. I could no longer struggle to wake up and go to the gym for exercises. I was more focused on my goals, and therefore I achieved more. I have learned to exercise willpower and have a successful life. I came to realize that willpower is learned by practicing more often. You should not beat yourself when you realize that you lack the willpower to do something. Many people go through the same. What you should do is resist that temptation as much as you can. It may take a long time to overcome it, but if you persist, you will win. You will discover after you overcome your urge to eat unhealthy food, your willpower will start being stronger.

How Do You Discipline Your Eating Habit?

Set Realistic Goals

One mistake that people make when setting their goals is setting targets that are unattainable. You cannot wake up one morning and say that you will give up on the food that you have been eating for a long time instantly. It will only lead to frustration, and there is a high probability that you will give up. Let us have an example of exercising. It will be unrealistic to imagine that you can do exercises seven days a week when you are just starting out. However, you can manage to exercise four or five days a week. Instead of starting to eat all the things that you don't like, you can start by introducing one food at a time. Have short term targets that will make it easy to attain your long –term targets.

For instance, when losing weight, have in place Small targets that you would like to hit before going for your larger goal. You can purpose to lose two pounds per week and then increase a pound in the subsequent weeks. This will keep you motivated to step up towards attaining your main goal.

Keep Away the Food You Want to Avoid

It is easier than the next thing you will grab and eat is just in front of you. Imagine your kitchen is filled with foods that you want to avoid such as snacks and sugary foods. It will be easy for you to be tempted to eat them. Therefore, keeping them from your reach will help greatly in ensuring that you don't eat them. Fill your kitchen with foods that are healthy. Even if you don't like eating them, you will have no choice but to eat them.

Ensure Your Kitchen is Clean

I know this may sound crazy, but it is true. Eating entails a lot of self-discipline and self-control. The environment that you are in will determine how your minds perform. When you keep your kitchen messy, you are likely to eat more than if when in a clean environment. When in a clean environment your minds will be focused and organized, and you will be mindful of what you are eating.

Therefore, it is important no matter the kind of environment you are, ensure it is clean because it will help your mind to stay organized so that you can stay away from unnecessary cravings.

Unfollow Pages That Promote the Foods That You Are Avoiding

Today the internet can determine what you eat. Imagine you are following pages on the internet that are advocating the same foods you are trying to avoid. It will only worsen your struggle towards eating what you don't like. It is like watching porn videos and at the same time say that you are abstaining. It will be shockingly impossible. Therefore, if you want to eat healthily, start away from reading things that promote those foods that you are trying to avoid.

Your brain is affected by what you see and therefore if you want to win the war of unhealthy eating, follow pages and accounts that promote the kind of foods that you are trying to eat. Remember you are eating what you don't like and so keeping away from other foods that you like will greatly help.

Look for Your Motivation

This is so important when working towards your diet. Why are you eating food that you don't like? By answering this question, you will be motivated to continue pushing through. You are not doing this for the sake of punishing yourself. You may be working towards losing weight, staying healthy and more importantly build your self-discipline. Review your reasons for doing it and stick to it. Be specific in what you want and write it down. The main reason why people give up is because they forget their goal of doing something. Reminding yourself this reason will help you to refuse temptations to give up.

Avoid Stress

Stress is one of the reasons that cause you to eat foods that are not healthy. This is because when under stress you are not able to control yourself properly. You cannot imagine yourself eating what you don't like when you are a victim of stress. Stress takes control of a person that you no longer pay close attention to what is good or bad. This could be among the reasons why some people indulge in smoking and alcohol drinking when under stress. Despite knowing the harm smoking can cause, they still do it.

Therefore, being stress-free is significant in choosing what to eat and not to eat. Avoiding stress will enable you have more control of your life. You can reduce stress by practicing mindfulness, having enough sleep and eating healthy. After this, you will be able to eat food that you don't like for the sake of gaining self-discipline.

Exercise Mindfulness While Choosing Food and When Consuming

This means that before you consume any food, spend some time and think fully about it. Ask yourself, is this what my body requires, or it is just one of your cravings? This will allow you to choose what you eat well after you have considered all the benefits and consequences.

If you find that despite liking a certain food, it will have long-lasting effects on your health, it will better to stop eating it. On the contrary, if there is a food that you hate, but it will work on your benefit, you will have no choice but to take it.

When you have decided on what to eat, don't be in a hurry while eating. You should experience pleasure while eating your food and so take the food slowly. When you exercise mindfulness while eating, it will not be easy to be addicted to food, and you will be proud concerning the food you have decided to eat, making you want to take it once more. Through this, you will find it easy to take that food more and more even though you didn't like it in the beginning.

The key to having self-discipline is doing the things we don't like so that you can achieve your goals. It may be that you don't like waking up early and do exercises or even practice mindfulness before going to your formal duties. But, looking at the benefits that will come from having such a habit, it will be right to give up on your sleep and do the right thing. Just like eating what you don't like for the sake of your health, you should go out of your comfort zone so that you can achieve your goals.

Your mind and your body will not always agree with what you must do, but you must ensure they do through exercise. When you have a clear picture of your expectations, don't let anything stand in your way. Don't be an enemy of yourself. Don't put hurdles for yourself when it is time to act. Sometimes your mind might tell that you are sacrificing your joy today because of what is unknown tomorrow, but you should not give in. Focus on your dreams more than you focus on your short-term pleasure, and you will see results.

Do not procrastinate on your dreams. Procrastination will deny you your opportunity to achieve greatness. Eliminate all distractions in your life and make sure each day you are making a step towards your achieving your goals.

If you find this book helpful in anyway a review to support my endeavors is much appreciated.

Edgar D. Moranis

I Will Teach You to Master Self-Discipline

www.ingramcontent.com/pod-product-compliance
Lightning Source LLC
Chambersburg PA
CBHW060453080526
44584CB00015B/1427